LOST RAILWAYS
OF
LINCOLNSHIRE

LOST RAILWAYS
OF
LINCOLNSHIRE

Alan Stennett

COUNTRYSIDE BOOKS
NEWBURY, BERKSHIRE

First published 2007
© Alan Stennett, 2007

COUNTRYSIDE BOOKS
3 Catherine Road
Newbury, Berkshire

To view our complete range of books,
please visit us at
www.countrysidebooks.co.uk

*To Marian, Ian and Alex,
with apologies for all the old railways
they were forced to walk in their childhood.*

ISBN 978 1 84674 040 4

The cover picture shows the A4 Class *Sir Nigel Gresley* under
the Cross 'O' Cliff Hill Bridge, having been diverted from the
East Coast mainline onto the Lincoln to Grantham line
and is from an original painting by
Colin Doggett

Designed by Mon Mohan
Produced through MRM Associates Ltd., Reading
Typeset by CJWT Solutions, St Helens
Printed by Cambridge University Press

*All material for the manufacture of this book
was sourced from sustainable forests.*

CONTENTS

ACKNOWLEDGEMENTS

The Great Northern Railway Society.
The Lincoln Railway Society.
The staff of Lincolnshire and NE Lincolnshire libraries.
The late George Holden and Geraldine Hill.
Percy Carter, the Winter family, Alf Mettam, David Skinns, Patrick Newton, Maurice and Denis Andrews, and many more railway and ex-railway staff and others who have visited Woodhall Junction and told us about life on the lines.

ABBREVIATIONS

The following abbreviations are used in this book:

AJR	Axholme Joint Railway
B&E	Bourne & Essendine Railway
DMU	Diesel Multiple Unit
E&M	Eastern & Midlands Railway
ECML	East Coast Main Line
ELR	East Lincolnshire Railway
FLR	Fleet Light Railway
G&IER	Grimsby & Immingham Electric Railway
G&MLR	Goole & Marshland Light Railway
GC	Great Central Railway
GE	Great Eastern Railway
GG&SJR	Great Grimsby & Sheffield Junction Railway
GN	Great Northern Railway
GN&GE	Great Northern & Great Eastern Joint Line
HKJRC	Horncastle & Kirkstead Junction Railway Company
IALR	Isle of Axholme Light Railway
L&ECR	Louth & East Coast Railway
L&Y	Lancashire & Yorkshire Railway
LD&EC	Lancashire, Derbyshire & East Coast Railway
LMS	London, Midland & Scottish Railway
LNER	London & North Eastern Railway
LNWR	London & North Western Railway
M&GN	Midland & Great Northern Joint Railway
MS&L	Manchester, Sheffield & Lincolnshire Railway
NLLR	North Lindsey Light Railway
S&E	Stamford & Essendine Railway Company
S&LJ	Sheffield & Lincolnshire Junction Railway
S&W	Sutton & Willoughby Railway

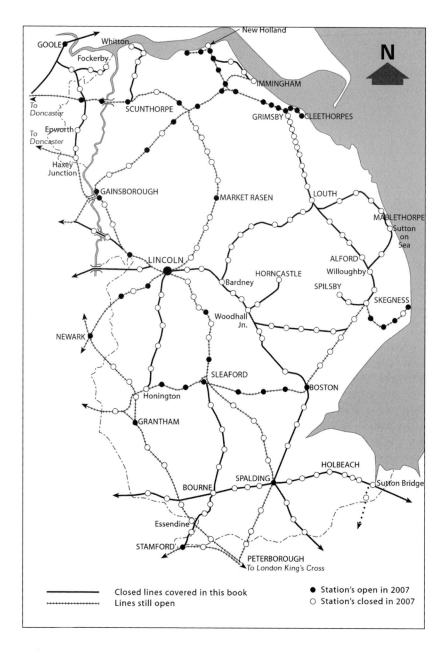

GOOLE
Whitton
Fockerby
New Holland
IMMINGHAM
To Doncaster
SCUNTHORPE
GRIMSBY CLEETHORPES
Epworth
To Doncaster
Haxey Junction
GAINSBOROUGH
MARKET RASEN
LOUTH
MABLETHORPE
Sutton on Sea
ALFORD
LINCOLN
HORNCASTLE
Willoughby
Bardney
SPILSBY
SKEGNESS
Woodhall Jn.
NEWARK
SLEAFORD
Honington
BOSTON
GRANTHAM
HOLBEACH
SPALDING
BOURNE
Sutton Bridge
Essendine
STAMFORD
PETERBOROUGH
To London King's Cross

N

——————— Closed lines covered in this book
·················· Lines still open

● Station's open in 2007
○ Station's closed in 2007

9

Introduction

At the start of the railway age more than three-quarters of the total population of Lincolnshire (100,000) lived in villages or the countryside. There were only two large towns, Lincoln itself and Boston, although Stamford, Grantham, Louth and Spalding were growing steadily. Hardly anybody lived in Grimsby in 1800, but the first enclosed dock was built in 1801, after which it grew rapidly. The population more than doubled between 1841 and 1851, and it became the largest town in the county by 1881. This expansion was driven by the massive increase in its fishing fleet, enticed there by railway company subsidies, and dock improvements, again largely railway company investments.

The lack of other potential customers meant that railways came late to Lincolnshire. In early plans, lines from London northwards passed through the county, and the first to be built, from Newark to Lincoln in 1846, was partly designed by the Midland Railway to block such proposals. This line crossed the most likely north–south routes, and the Midland hoped to control the traffic from Lincoln, seen as the only significant centre.

Two north–south lines were eventually built through the county to the north: the Great Northern Railway's line, still in use as the East Coast Main Line (ECML), and the Joint Line operated by the Great Northern and the Great Eastern. The Great Northern also built the Lincolnshire Loop Line: parts of it are still in use, but most is gone.

Two lines set out to serve Grimsby. The East Lincolnshire Railway (ELR), from Boston, is no more, but the Manchester, Sheffield & Lincolnshire Railway's line (MS&L) from Doncaster is still a key rail route, having grown with the steel industry at Scunthorpe and the port and industrial facilities at Immingham, largely developed by the railway company. The MS&L, later the Great Central (GC), also served the ferries from New Holland to Hull, a business that remained in railway hands until the opening of the Humber Bridge in 1980.

LNER 0-6-0 No 8175 passing through Spalding. (R.K. Blencowe)

The rest of the county was mainly served by local lines, often promoted by landowners and traders anxious about the decline of their market town when the main lines missed it. Some were built with hopes of becoming part of a major through-route. Many never got Parliamentary approval, although the proposed 'Bridge-end, Burton Pedwardine, Scredington, Three Queens and Midland Junction Railway', advertised in the *Stamford Mercury* by Messrs Bubble and Squeak of Scredington and Mr Timothy Teazer from Burton Pedwardine, probably never expected it!

The lines that were built generally served their communities well, helping achieve 'the annihilation of time and space' for goods and passengers of which the *Stamford Mercury* so approved in 1848. Many made good profits in the early years carrying coal, timber, manure, roadstone, bricks, tiles and other commodities into the county, and taking away grain, vegetables, potatoes, cut flowers, livestock and other agricultural produce.

Passenger traffic was always important, but came second to goods on most inland lines, some of which closed to passengers

11

in the 1930s. The most important exception was the seaside holiday-maker. Occasions such as the Lancashire Wakes Weeks, when a whole town shut down for several days, provided an opportunity to get away, and Sunday outings organised by people like Thomas Cook from Leicester became popular. The lines to Cleethorpes, Skegness, Mablethorpe and Sutton on Sea all found visitors and day-trippers profitable customers, and the GC invested heavily to develop Cleethorpes.

You can still take a train for a day by the sea at Cleethorpes and 'Skeggy', but not to Mablethorpe or Sutton, and lines built to speed the holiday-maker to the coast have been lost. Hobbled by the need to publish a price for every traffic, and blocked by law from offering a better deal to particular customers, the goods trade was gradually poached by lorry owners, and the passengers moved onto buses and, eventually, private cars.

The railways also suffered from a lack of political support. State funding often had to be directed to catching up on under-

An excursion headed by a B1 4-6-0 enters Woodhall Junction.

investment in previous years, and was usually concentrated on the main lines and inter-city routes, few of which run through Lincolnshire. The secondary routes and branches were left to fade away.

My own interest in railways began with two such lines. I was brought up in the village of Billingborough, where the branch line had closed to passengers in the 1930s, but where the daily goods train gave a small boy a glimpse of a grubby black 0-6-0 loco with a few trucks. The interest was rekindled in 1992, when my wife Sue and I moved into the old station house at what had been Woodhall Junction station. That had been a more important line, carrying everything from a queen to coffins. The more we found out about its history, and how it tied in to the rest of the Lincolnshire railway network, the more interested we became.

That kind of line forms the bulk of this book. Some went before the Second World War, others would probably have gone if they had not had a vital role during the conflict, but the closures began again in the 1950s, to culminate in the 1960s. In this book, that pattern of initial enthusiasm, local support, agricultural traffic and good profits, followed by years of under-investment, lost business and final closure, will be taken for granted. We will concentrate on local issues for the lines concerned.

Alan Stennett

1
The Lincolnshire Loop Line

The Lincolnshire Loop Line, which ran from Peterborough to Doncaster by way of Lincoln, was part of the Great Northern (GN) Railway's plans to link Yorkshire and Lincolnshire to London. The company's 'Towns' line, from King's Cross to Doncaster, passing through Grantham, Newark and Retford, is still with us as the East Coast Main Line (ECML), but much of the Loop has been lost.

It was an important line to the county because it linked a number of local communities. It remains in service between Peterborough and Spalding, although the intermediate stations at Peakirk, Deeping St James and Littleworth have all been closed. From Spalding the line continued across the Fens, through Surfleet, Algarkirk & Sutterton and Kirton, before crossing the Witham at Boston on the Grand Sluice Bridge. Turning onto the east bank of the river it followed it to Lincoln, passing through Langrick, Dogdyke, Tattershall, Kirkstead (later renamed Woodhall Junction), Stixwould, Southrey, Bardney, Washingborough and Five Mile House on its way to the city. All of this section is now closed. North of Lincoln, the line continued to Doncaster, and is still in use as part of what became the GN&GE Joint line.

The Loop was completed in 1848, four years before the Towns line. Track on the Boston–Lincoln section was laid on the banks of the Witham, a navigation channel which the GN owned but 'allowed' to run down. To assist in that process, several cattle wagons were converted into standing-only 'fourth-class' passenger vehicles with fares of 1/3d. That was intended to be cheap enough to tempt passengers away from the packet boats, small steam ships or sailing barges which had been the main

Train leaving Boston over the Grand Sluice Bridge, once the entry point to the East Lincolnshire lines, now just a branch to Skegness. (Peter Grey collection)

transport hitherto. Building on company-owned land kept purchase costs down, but meant the route followed a rather winding course.

The opening was marked by a variety of celebrations in Boston, including tea and buns for 2,500 children, a tea-party and lecture on steam propulsion for several hundred members of the 'working classes', and a ride on the train followed by 'a grand dinner' for the 4–500 people who could afford the 8/6d tickets. A total of 21 toasts were drunk at the dinner, and GN director Edmund Dennison claimed that the line would prove 'of imperishable and lasting' benefit to the town and to Lincolnshire. History does not record how well he managed 'imperishable and lasting' after 21 toasts.

16

Bardney station at the opening of the line in 1848.

Between 1848 and 1852, the Loop was the main GN line to the North, and carried Queen Victoria on at least one occasion, probably in 1850. It is reported that, when a group of civic dignitaries arrived at Lincoln station to meet her, she refused to leave the train. Apparently she had vowed not to set foot in the city while its MP, Colonel Charles Sibthorp, held the seat, and she kept her word. The reason was that, on the eve of Victoria's marriage to her beloved Prince Albert, Col Sibthorp had voted against an allowance of £50,000 a year to be paid to the prince, remarking in the House of Commons that £30,000 would have been 'more than enough for a foreign prince'. Col Sibthorp presumably was not too concerned, since he hated anything to do with railways, and voted against all Parliamentary bills proposing them. His confidence appears to have been well founded, since Lincoln continued to return him to Westminster until his death, after which they elected his son.

For about the same period, Boston was the engineering headquarters of the GN, but the need to have that facility on the main line saw it removed in 1853 to what became the famous Doncaster Works. The driving force behind the move was Edmund Dennison, vice-chairman of the GN, whose home was in Doncaster. The works later produced the great steam locomotives designed by Sir Nigel Gresley, including the world steam speed record holder *Mallard* and the legendary *Flying Scotsman*.

The coming of the railway was also a benefit to bright young men wanting to escape from a life on the land. A railway job was more secure and better paid, although few of the staff got rich on the wages. Retired railwayman George Holden talked to me about working in 1921/2 at Woodhall Junction, or Kirkstead as it was at the time. He told us that, when he joined the GN two stations down the line at Dogdyke in 1920, he was paid the princely sum of £10/6d a week as a junior clerk – not much for what was quite a responsible job on a small country station.

'Those were hard times,' he remembered. 'I didn't get onto the staff for another three years, and that was only after going to London for a written examination, a full medical and an interview with the directors. I had to stand in front of the table for the whole of that meeting, and they looked at you as if you were a lower form of life! I can also remember getting a telegram one Friday, telling me go to another station fifty miles away on the Monday, and that was a permanent move.' Sadly, Mr Holden died recently, at the age of 99.

Following the brief spell of glory at the opening, the line settled down to a more humdrum existence as part rural railway, part mainline link. Peterborough to Boston was an important stretch, as the continuation of the East Lincolnshire Railway, carrying fast passenger and goods trains, particularly fish, from Grimsby to London, and will be considered in more detail with that line.

North of Lincoln the Loop was, and remains, a route to the North, and, until the closure of most of the mines, an artery for Yorkshire coal heading south. From Boston to Lincoln, the line also carried coal, but that function was reduced by the opening of the GN&GE Joint line (see Chapter 10), which offered a direct route from Lincoln to Spalding and on to March and London.

The sleeper treatment depot at Hall Hills, just to the north of Lincoln, also saw regular traffic. Untreated timber sleepers were delivered to the depot, where they were placed in huge cylindrical tanks and immersed in a creosote solution under

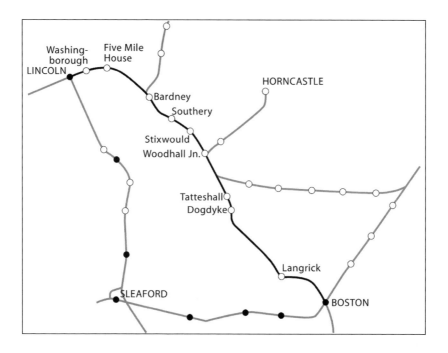

pressure. This preserved the wood, making it less prone to attack by insects or the weather, and treated sleepers were shipped out to the rest of the system through to 1965, despite a major fire which destroyed much of the works in 1957. The use of concrete sleepers eventually removed the need for the depot, but old railway sleepers are still valuable on farms and in gardens for their ability to resist the weather.

The sugar beet factory at Bardney was a major user of the line. The plant was built in 1925 as part of the expansion of processing beet for sugar that began in Britain shortly after the First World War. Two other factories were built in Lincolnshire, at Brigg and Spalding. The process involved chopping, boiling and treating the beet root with a variety of processes to extract the sugar. Huge tonnages of beet were moved during the 'campaign', as it is still known, and large amounts of coal were needed to drive the machinery and boil the 'juices'. Sugar, beet

2-6-0 No 43109 passes the cannery at Bardney with a mixed goods train.
(Great Northern Railway Society – Rod Knight)

pulp for animal feed and a variety of other products also needed to be taken away from the factory, so it was vital to have good rail links to carry the materials and transport the people who were employed there. Alf Mettam, who worked at Bardney in the 1930s, recalls that six trains were needed at the change of each shift to carry the workers to and from Lincoln.

This section was liable to flooding. One goods train driver recalled that he and the fireman had no trouble as their engine passed through a flooded section, but the guard had to stand on his seat in the brake van as the water flowed in through the door at the front and out again at the rear. Another commented on the 'sport' of throwing lumps of coal at the geese on the river bank at Kirkstead while their early morning trains were being watered at Woodhall Junction. It is not recorded whether anyone scored a hit, but the owners of the birds doubtless gratefully collected the free fuel.

The closeness to the river was also a benefit to the many

Tattershall station. (Great Northern Railway Society)

fishermen who travelled down from Sheffield and elsewhere for days out or for the competitions, known as matches, which were held on the banks. The stretches along the Witham at Kirkstead, Tattershall and Dogdyke were particularly good for matches, since the competitors could have very similar 'pegs' – marked spots for each fisherman – along a long stretch of riverbank with very similar conditions, giving no one too much advantage from their position. Fishing was an enormously popular pastime between the World Wars and into the 1960s, with hundreds and sometimes thousands of fishermen and spectators travelling to suitable locations – it usually was men, although wives and children sometimes came along for a day out by the river.

On one occasion six special trains were held in Woodhall Junction yard during a match at Kirkstead, waiting to take everyone back home again at the end of the day. Bookmakers travelled down in the trains, taking bets on the matches, then retired to a room at the King's Head to sort the takings in preparation for paying out again on the way back.

The station and ferry at Dogdyke in the 1930s.

Matches were often sponsored by breweries, and one story tells how the train travelled slowly down the riverside, with the fishermen jumping out close to their pegs, and waiting for a bottle of beer to be handed down from the guard's compartment as it passed by. Competitions still take place today, but the participants come down by car, and there are not nearly as many of them.

All the stations between Boston and Lincoln were to be 'plain and inexpensive' according to the original plans, but that didn't prevent the architect from indulging in some Italianate fancies, and three-storey towers with elaborate brickwork and overhanging roofs featured at many of the larger ones.

Each station was situated close to a bridge or ferry. A bridge was already in existence at Tattershall; the GN paid for a swing bridge to be constructed at Kirkstead and contributed half of the cost of a conventional one at Bardney. A bridge replaced the ferry at Langrick in 1899 but Washingborough,

The timber bridge originally constructed to carry the line over the river Witham at Bardney.

Five Mile House, Southrey, Stixwould and Dogdyke continued to be served by ferries up to, and sometimes after, the closure of the line. The crossing at Dogdyke was particularly busy at train times, since the village lay on the opposite side of the river to the station, and that at Southrey ensured the water supply for a family on the fen side as late as the 1960s. No water pipe ran to their house, so a son brought two empty buckets with him on the way to school. On the way home, he filled them from the tap in the station toilets and took the water home for the following day's supply.

Since the whole river navigation was owned by the GN, the ferries, and the swing bridge, were their responsibility, and railway staff operated them where necessary.

Washingborough Ferry was the scene of an unfortunate accident during the First World War. A train had been attacked in the cutting there by an enemy airship, which dropped bombs but missed the train, although the driver's hair is reported to have turned white during the attack. The following day large numbers of people boarded the ferry to look at the bomb damage, but the numbers crowding on caused it to turn over, drowning a young man and a child. The rest of the passengers were taken to Washingborough station, where they were given blankets and put on a special train to Lincoln.

Two bridges on the line, the Grand Sluice bridge at Boston and the one at Bardney were initially built of timber, but, after a fire destroyed one elsewhere, the company decided they were not suitable for the long term, and replaced them with more conventional structures.

As well as local and through traffic, the Loop was served by the Horncastle and Louth branches which joined at Kirkstead and Bardney respectively. This section also carried many excursion trains and specials heading for the seaside. Initially, these ran from Lincoln to Boston, returning up the East Lincolnshire Line to connect with the coastal branches, but in 1913 the opening of the New Line, from Kirkstead to Firsby, meant they only used the Loop as far as Coningsby Junction, before heading out across the fens.

Kirkstead station played a role in an ecclesiastical scandal in 1921. The Archdeacon of Stow was accused of having been in a hotel room in Peterborough with a woman, but offered as an alibi that he had stopped off at Kirkstead to meet the Deacon of St Leonard's Chapel on the platform. The Deacon was never called, so the story was not tested, but the Archdeacon was removed from office.

The line saw heavy use during the Second World War when it acted as a diversionary route for goods away from the ECML and the Joint Line, as well as serving the RAF stations at Bardney, Woodhall Spa and Coningsby. Crews, bombs, fuel and ammunition were brought in, but there was also outgoing traffic. One lady porter at Woodhall Junction told me how upset she had been at the sight of the coffins of dead airmen being loaded into a goods van at the station. Another van was held at Dogdyke station for the same purpose, but the news reaching there wasn't always bad. A bicycle owned by an airman missing on a raid was kept at the station for six months, then sent off to London for disposal. Shortly afterwards, the airman's parents

Langrick station. (Great Northern Railway Society)

were in touch – he was a prisoner of war, and could they have his bike back!

The bend of the line close to the Witham at Langrick was one of the stabling points for a large naval gun mounted on a railway wagon, kept ready to defend the Lincolnshire coast against invasion. It is believed that the location was chosen because extensive tree cover offered some protection against detection and attack by German aircraft. The stations on the line did receive some attention from enemy aircraft; a signalman at Woodhall Junction kept the bullet he dug out of the woodwork of the signal box after one such visit.

Closures on this part of the Loop began in 1963, when the section between Coningsby Junction and Boston, with the stations at Tattershall, Dogdyke and Langrick all closing on 17 June. The remaining stretch, from Lincoln to Coningsby Junction, closed to passengers on the same date as much of the rest of the East Lincolnshire system: 5 October 1970. For a short while, much of the line remained open to allow a diesel shunter with one or two tank wagons and a brake van to serve an agricultural depot in Horncastle, but this trade ended in April 1971, leaving only the section from Lincoln to the British Sugar factory at Bardney to see an occasional coal train to the works. This too had closed by the 1980s.

Most of the line is easy to follow, since a Sustrans cycle path has been established along much of the route. It follows the old trackbed past Washingborough station, now a private house, continues through the site of Five Mile House, at which nothing remains, and continues over the Witham bridge into Bardney. The station building at Bardney was demolished in the 1990s, and the materials were taken to Peterborough, with the intention of re-erecting it as part of the Museum of World Railways, but the goods shed is intact, and has also been converted into a dwelling. The cycle path deviates from the line to go round the now-closed British Sugar factory, but soon rejoins it to continue through the sites of Southrey and Stixwould stations, to Woodhall Junction. Platforms can still be seen at both the intermediate stations, and the signal box and stationmaster's

Kirkstead station in about 1900. The station was renamed Woodhall Junction in 1922.

26

Woodhall Junction now. (Author)

house at Stixwould have been converted into an attractive house and religious retreat.

Woodhall Junction is our home, and we have tried to maintain the original appearance as much as possible. Both platforms are currently intact and the brick station buildings have been incorporated into, as an early GN document describes it, 'the C-in-C's residence' (Clerk in Charge, an early post that was superior to that of the stationmaster). A board outside the station shows pictures of it in its working days, and gives a potted history of the location.

From Woodhall Junction onwards the cycle path leaves the

27

line, and crosses Kirkstead Bridge to the opposite bank, since much of the trackbed is privately owned from here to Dogdyke. However, the station at Tattershall can be seen from the Tattershall–Sleaford road, and can sometimes be visited, since it operates as a gallery for the resident artist. The site of Dogdyke station can also be found, with some buildings intact, by taking the road from Coningsby. Do not be confused by the fact that Dogdyke itself is on the opposite side of the river. The absence of a ferry nowadays could leave you with a frustratingly distant view.

If you are need refreshment, then visit Langrick station, which now serves as a roadside café. The cycle route rejoins the line near here, having crossed back over Langrick Bridge, and continues into Boston, passing the site of the Hall Hills sleeper depot, now a caravan and leisure park.

2
Fast Fish

The East Lincolnshire Railway

The East Lincolnshire Railway did exactly what it said in its Act – it served the towns and villages of East Lincolnshire with a fast, reliable rail service on a well engineered 47-mile double track main line.

At first the company was closely associated with the GN, with two directors on both boards. The list of backers included an earl, two lords and much of the Lincolnshire squirearchy. The promoters emphasised the benefit to 'graziers and cattle feeders' of 'cheap and ready access' to markets in London and the North. In return, they expected cheaper coal, building materials, fertilisers and 'manufactured goods and articles of merchandise'.

They also noted that the famous Wolds wool could be delivered to the Yorkshire markets without 'the tedious and expensive carriage by water'. Some would have gone to Lincoln, then by barge along the Fossdyke Navigation, the Trent and the Ouse, but that from east of the Wolds would have had to be carted to Louth, put onto a barge to the coast, transhipped into a bigger vessel for the journey along the coast and through the Humber estuary, and sometimes transhipped again at Goole or onto one of the canals which served Yorkshire industry.

One accurate prediction in the prospectus was that the line would win an important business in transporting fish from the rapidly expanding port of Grimsby to London and the South.

Although the ELR remained an independent – and profitable – company up to the 1923 Grouping of all the railway companies in Britain into the London & North Eastern (LNER), the London, Midland & Scottish (LMS), Great Western (GWR) and Southern (SR) Railways, throughout its existence the line was leased and operated by the GN and its successors.

The crew of GN 0-4-2 tank No 126 pose with other railway staff on the loco at Alford station. (From the Museum of Lincolnshire Life, by courtesy of Lincolnshire County Council)

Planned to run from Grimsby to Boston, where it would connect with the GN's Lincolnshire Loop line, the line was opened in stages. The first trains ran over the fourteen miles between Louth and Grimsby in March 1848, although a special train had made the journey six months earlier. Trains then continued over MS&L lines to the Humber ferries at New Holland. The line from Louth to Boston was completed by 1 October 1848, with the GN Lincolnshire Loop Line to Peterborough opening a few days later, allowing connections there for London and the South, with through trains to the capital possible a few months later when the GN line to London was completed.

What became the East Lincolnshire Main Line then consisted of the ELR and the southern section of the Lincolnshire Loop,

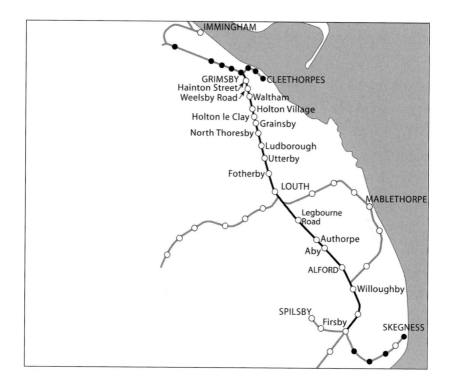

serving the market towns of Louth, Alford, Burgh-le-Marsh, Boston and Spalding, with stops at Waltham, Holton-le-Clay, North Thoresby and Ludborough between Grimsby and Louth. Several halts were added from 1905 as part of an experimental steam railcar service. Legbourne Road, Authorpe, and Aby & Claythorpe – Aby was the shortest signal-box name in Britain – were on the way to Alford; and Willoughby before Burgh-le-Marsh.

After Alford came the imposing structure of Firsby, fully roofed, like Louth and Alford, but serving a tiny community. In later years the branches to Spilsby and Skegness were built, but did the ELR plan for them? The station originally boasted a wooden goods shed, but in 1860 this, and the one at Louth, blew away in a storm and both were replaced with more conventional

Firsby station. (Peter Grey)

GN structures. Four stations, all now closed, were on the line linking Firsby to Boston, with Kirton, Algarkirk & Sutton and Surfleet between Boston and Spalding. On the final stretch before Peterborough trains stopped at Littleworth, Deeping St James and Peakirk.

In addition to the branches joining at Firsby, the ELR also connected with other GN-controlled lines coming in from the seaside resorts of Mablethorpe and Sutton on Sea; across the Wolds from Bardney to Louth, and, from 1913, across the Fens from Coningsby. Few places in the east of the county were not served by the line or its connections.

One location which lost those services was New Holland, because, shortly after opening, a dispute broke out between the GN and the MS&L. The two companies had an agreement under which MS&L trains could run over GN lines to Louth and GN trains over MS&L tracks to New Holland. The MS&L had allied itself with other companies, including the London & North

C12 tank No 67364 at Louth station in 1955. (R.K. Blencowe)

Western, which was worried about competition for London business from trains running into the GN's King's Cross. The allies wanted to block the GN's route north via the Humber ferries, so the MS&L tried to stop trains going through to the pier. Lines were blocked in Grimsby to prevent trains getting through, and fights broke out between the companies' employees. Even when a GN train did get through, the MS&L often sent the ferry away early to ensure passengers missed their connections. The GN eventually gave up the struggle, and passengers had to change to MS&L trains in Grimsby. In return, the MS&L ceased to use their rights to run trains along the ELR.

Most of the initial predictions for the line proved accurate, with agricultural produce carried in large amounts, particularly grain and potatoes, and sugar beet important once the industry became established between the First and Second World Wars. Livestock, particularly cattle, did leave the county for various markets, but much also came in to be fattened up on the rich grazing lands near the coast.

Fish proved very important, after Grimsby became the largest fishing port in the country. The docks were largely built by the MS&L, and the GN enticed a group of fishing-boat owners to move from the South Coast and base themselves in the new facilities. The GN won a large part of the fish trade, especially in the early years, but rising popularity of fish and chips in the 1900s saw some of this trade taken by the GC, successor to the MS&L. The GC supplied the industrial North and Midlands, but at least two fast fish trains a day ran over the ELR to London for most of its existence. Their diversion via Doncaster in the 1960s has been seen as one of the indications of closure for the line.

One rather surprising traffic from the 1930s was iron ore from near Grantham to the steelworks at Scunthorpe. This roundabout journey was used to reduce congestion on the ECML, which was the most direct route.

The line also carried water for a brief period, when old locomotive tenders were used to carry fresh water from Willoughby to Lincoln, during the typhoid epidemic of 1905.

Passenger transport was vitally important, mainly due to a factor that the promoters had not taken into account: the seaside visitor and holiday-maker. The branches to Skegness, Mablethorpe and Sutton on Sea carried millions of trippers, all

The train of locomotive tenders that carried water from Willoughby to Lincoln during the typhoid outbreak of 1905. (Great Northern Railway Society)

of whom arrived over the ELR. It has been estimated that over 100,000 visited Skegness alone in 1880, and on August Bank Holiday 1882 so many visitors arrived that the railway did not get them all away again until after 2 am the following day, by which time the famished hordes had eaten and drunk everything available in the town, leaving it 'as bare of nutriments as was Egypt after the visitation of the locusts' according to a local paper. Visitor numbers at Skegness rose to over 700,000 a year by 1938, but by then few went hungry.

In 1849, every day except Sundays six passenger trains ran each way, and this rose to eight each way by the 1920s, with additional services between Louth and Grimsby, some going on to Mablethorpe. Up to seven goods trains ran a day, with the two fast fish trains treated in all respects as expresses. The straight, level lines meant that good speeds could be maintained, even by smaller engines, and the ELR became a happy hunting ground for the GN's beautiful single-wheelers and Atlantics as they were displaced from the ECML by more powerful locomotives. Bigger locos were needed for heavy goods trains, and anything, including the 9F 2-10-0, British Rail's last steam design, could be found on the line in its later days.

Trains were not always fast. During the General Strike of 1926, one arrived in Boston from Grimsby manned by two students and a vicar. They had demolished several sets of crossing gates on their way, and taken seven hours to make a journey that normally required about two, even for a stopping train.

Services slowed to a halt on parts of the line during the snows of 1947. A cattle train was snowed in at one point, and a farmer had to be employed to take feed to the animals. Drifts more than fifteen feet deep had to be dug away before trains were able to move again. One railwayman working on a drift reported that he had dug down several feet before he came to the top of a telegraph pole, showing how far he still had to go. Percy Carter, a railwayman in charge of some of the work, climbed a signal post in a snowstorm but could not get down again until a fireman blew the accumulated snow away with the steam pipe from the footplate. 'If it had been a diesel, I would still have been there,' he commented.

Clearing snow drifts from the line near Louth during the winter of 1947.

After the Second World War the East Lincolnshire lost traffic to buses and lorries, like most railways serving rural areas. Some smaller halts closed, particularly those built before the war for the railcar service. Seventeen stations lost passenger service in 1963, and twenty-two goods yards closed the following year, but nobody expected the wholesale slaughter proposed in the Beeching report. The Doctor recommended that the entire ELR and all the branches that it served should go. The relatively flat line, with few gradients, and some of the longest straight runs on British railways, meant lots of level crossings, each with its crossing keeper. Substantial savings could be made simply by doing away with the crossing keepers!

Some may have been pleased to go. A crossing keeper's life saw long hours, low pay and basic living conditions. The daughter of one described being brought up in a house with two rooms upstairs and two down for the whole family, no running water and very spartan bathing and toilet facilities. 'The whole

GN railmotor No 8 at Louth station. (Great Northern Railway Society – Eric Neve)

family had a bath in a tin bath in the back kitchen on a Friday night,' she explained. 'That was the only day of the week that the front door was opened, because the butcher called on a Friday, and we couldn't let him in through the back.'

A successful campaign to keep the line to Skegness open meant that the ELR between Boston and a point just south of the station at Firsby was retained to serve the resort, but most of the rest of the line was closed in October 1970. Two sections stayed open as goods branches, serving the sugar beet factory at Spalding, and the local maltings at Louth (so keeping open the first part of the ELR to see service, Grimsby to Louth). Both sections closed in 1980, with the end of beet processing at Spalding and rail transport of grain to Louth.

At the northern end, the Grimsby and Louth Railway Preservation Society evolved from a group that had campaigned since 1978 for the restoration of passenger services. When British Rail withdrew, they tried to preserve the whole stretch, running a final special excursion between Louth and Grimsby to promote

GN Atlantic No 294 entering Ludborough station. (North East Lincolnshire Council Library Service)

Ludborough now: the Lincolnshire Wolds Railway. The loco pulling out of Ludborough is Peckett 0-4-0 Fulstow No 2. (Lincolnshire Wolds Railway)

the cause, but failed to raise enough money fast enough to do this. However, trading as The Great Northern and East Lincolnshire Railway plc, they established a base at Ludborough in 1984 and, at the time of writing, are about to complete laying track to North Thoresby. New roadworks at the Grimsby end have cut them off from a connection to the national network, but their plans envisage services between a new station in Louth and one at Waltham, on the outskirts of Grimsby.

To the surprise of most observers, another local campaign, supported by the local council, succeeded in getting the line from Peterborough to Spalding reopened in 1971, and it remains in business to this day.

Some closed sections of the line can be followed with relative ease today. On the stretch from Spalding to Boston, a new road linking the towns has been laid on the old trackbed. The stations at Kirton and Surfleet have been almost obliterated, with housing developments on the Kirton site and a single railway-style gate-post the only remnant at Surfleet. Algarkirk & Sutterton station and goods shed are virtually intact, with the station serving as a base for a training company and the goods shed formerly used by a transport firm (though I saw no activity there recently).

Hardly anything is left at Firsby: just the station house, with part of the old goods shed incorporated into a potato pack-house. Many of the stations from there to Grimsby can be located – although much of the track as far as Louth has been taken back into farmland – and road crossings often reveal themselves by the presence of a keeper's house. Remaining station or crossing keeper's houses are all in private hands, although that at Ludborough can be booked as a holiday cottage.

A section of trackbed between Bratoft and Burgh-le-Marsh, owned by the National Trust, is open as a footpath. The station at Burgh-le-Marsh is virtually intact, and is intermittently in use as a tea-room. The goods shed was the base for a railway museum, now closed. The trackbed just north of the station has now been cut by the bypass round the village.

Little remains now of Willougby station, the junction for the Sutton branch, although the location can be worked out with the use of a good map. The main station buildings at Alford are intact, being used as offices, although the overall roof has long gone. In a nice touch of irony, the approach road is now called 'Beechings Way'.

A fine group of arches at Claythorpe takes the line across the Great Eau and on to Aby station, where the stationmaster's house is lived in, and the goods shed is still in place. The stationmaster's house at Authorpe is also still lived in. Legbourne Road is in good condition, and was home to another railway museum, which closed in 1999. The large GN-style building adjacent to the house is not original, but was built for the museum.

The main station building at Louth was Grade 1-listed, and a battle took place after closure to prevent it being demolished. One campaigner described the developers as 'worse than the Germans', who had damaged the station with two bombs during the Second World War. A compromise was reached

Louth station in 1950. (R.K. Blencowe)

whereby the building was converted into apartments, and they can be found within the larger development. A signal box in Louth marks the start of the section of trackbed leased by the Preservation Society, and the line can be followed from here to Waltham, where it disappears under the new road developments.

Fotherby, Utterby, Grainsby and Holton Village halts were demolished by BR well before final closure, and little remains at any of them, but the bigger stations can still be located.

The preservation base at Ludborough is well worth a visit. They have had to rebuild virtually all the facilities, including a GN-style signal box, and are doing the same at North Thoresby. The Society operates several small steam and diesel locomotives, and is open most weekends, with trains running every other Sunday, as well as Santa Specials in December. Running days often coincide with other events on the site.

3
Ferries and Docks

The Grimsby and Immingham Electric Railway
The Barton and Immingham Light Railway
New Holland and the Humber ferries

The ports of Grimsby, Immingham and Barton-upon-Humber have long been linked by railways, and remain so today, but the area has lost three specialised railway lines.

The Grimsby and Immingham Electric Railway

This six-mile line ran from the docks in Immingham to Immingham Town station, where it reversed, then continued as a conventional railway line to the outskirts of Grimsby, at which point it became a street tramway to a terminus at Corporation Bridge.

The service was purely a passenger one, carrying dock workers to and from their work. It opened in 1912, with sixteen single-deck electric cars taking power from an overhead cable, although four were intended to operate over a link with the Grimsby tramway system, which was never established. They were withdrawn in the early 1930s. Originally the cars carried fully lined teak livery, but the work and the corrosive sea winds soon dulled the shine, and by the 1930s they had acquired a rather dull brown LNER livery. The tramway ran a 24-hour service, although car numbers increased substantially during shift changes, with some reports mentioning convoys of six cars running together.

Various nicknames attached to the service over the years. 'The

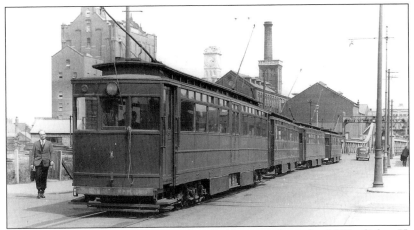

Trams at the Grimsby Corporation Bridge terminus in 1953. (John H. Meredith)

Clickety' came from the sound of the wheels on the track, but 'Rattlesnakes' was more from the sound and motion of the cars when they hit a top speed of nearly 30mph on the country sections. The four stops on this part of the route were all by request, and one traveller admitted that he often expected the car to overshoot the stop when he stepped out to wave the driver down.

A large industrial estate was developed between Grimsby and Immingham on land purchased by Grimsby Corporation during the Second World War, and laid out with roads and railway sidings. The area became the world's largest producer of titanium dioxide, an important constituent of paint, and fertiliser and textile plants soon arrived. The tramway purchased twenty second-hand cars immediately after the war to deal with the passengers to these new industries, but the closure of the street section in Grimsby made it much less useful.

Many travellers transferred to the buses, despite the fact that the journey took twice as long, and others bought cars. Costs on the tramway rose; revenue fell, and eventually it was decided not to replace them. The line closed in 1961. Ironically, this did

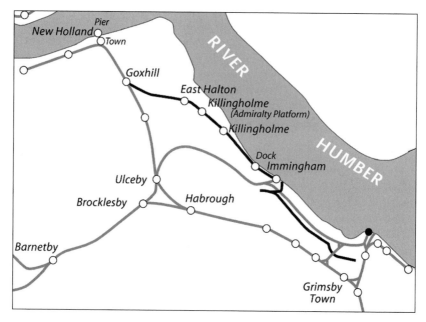

Repairing the track after the East Coast floods of 1953. (John H. Meredith)

not stem the losses, since many customers had previously held free tram passes, and British Rail was now obliged to buy tickets on the replacement bus services.

Three vehicles from the G&IER are preserved. Two of the later cars are still 'in service', one at the Beamish Museum near Durham and the other at the Tramway Museum at Crich, but both have reverted to their pre-G&IER Gateshead livery. Car 14, one of the original fleet, is preserved at Crich in the later BR livery, but only as a static exhibit.

Virtually nothing remains of the system today, although poles with fittings for the overhead wires can sometimes be found along the route, particularly near Immingham Docks.

The Barton and Immingham Light Railway

This seven-mile line, completed in 1911, was rather misnamed, since it never got to Barton and was not built as a light railway! As built, it ran from a junction at Goxhill (with the GC line to Barton-upon-Humber and the New Holland ferries) to a terminus at Immingham Docks, by way of stations at East Halton and Killingholme.

Despite its small size, and relative unimportance, East Halton did enter the history books when it was bombed by a Zeppelin during the First World War, making it one of the first railway targets to be bombed from the air. One local paper refers to people being 'terrified' by the 'huge machine' as it apparently headed for the steel works at Scunthorpe. The village was attacked twice by Zeppelins, but the only casualty was a calf, killed in the second raid.

The northern part of the line never carried much freight, and East Halton had no facilities to deal with goods traffic, but large amounts came in from the south to serve industries north of the main docks, which were encouraged by the GC in the early twentieth century. Passenger traffic was mainly workers at the docks and industries round Immingham, but the line also linked Immingham with Hull by way of the Humber ferries.

45

The track maintenance gang responsible for the upkeep of the Immingham –
Goxhill line on their trolley.

From left to right: Charlie Dixon, Bill Douglas (ganger), Aaron and Jack (?) Spittlehouse, Charley Lamming, Park Clayton, Herbert Dent and, standing, Goxhill stationmaster, Fred Dooley. (Ann Boulton)

Admiralty Platform halt near Killingholme. (North East Lincolnshire Council Library Service)

An additional halt was opened in 1921 to serve a small naval base, but Admiralty Platform halt had no facilities of any kind except the platform, with the result that no tickets were ever issued from it.

Diesel railcars came to the line relatively early, when the 'Derby Heavyweight' multiple units arrived in 1956. Although costs reduced, the line was not viable, and the section from Goxhill to Killingholme closed in 1963. It is still used for goods from Killingholme into Immingham.

The route of the closed part of the line can be seen at road crossings, and at the East Halton station site, where the platforms remain in a heavily overgrown cutting. The stationmaster's house is now a private residence.

New Holland and the Humber ferries

The section of railway that served the ferries across the Humber to Hull is less than a mile long, but carried two stations, at New Holland Town and New Holland Pier.

It was the northern extremity of the MS&L (later GC) branch from Grimsby, and for a brief period after opening in 1848, was part of a route from London to the North that ran via the East Lincolnshire Railway (see Chapter 2).

That moment of glory did not last long, since in 1852 the GN opened its direct line north via Newark and Doncaster and took away most of the through passengers, but the rail and ferry link across the Humber saved a 60-mile road journey, and it continued to serve the local communities for more than a century.

The ferries had been bought in 1846 by the Great Grimsby & Sheffield Junction Railway, part of the MS&L, for £21,000. Four years later it was discovered that a group of GG&SJR directors, knowing the railway's intentions, had bought the ferries themselves in 1845 for £10,000, pocketing a tidy profit from the later sale. They were compelled to pay this back, and those on the MS&L board lost their seats.

The ferries remained in railway ownership until rendered obsolete by the Humber Bridge in 1981. They were treated as a railway service: Hull Corporation Pier was counted as a railway station despite having no track. At their peak, they transported over 30,000 passengers, 1,000 head of livestock, 250 vehicles and more than 300 tons of merchandise every year.

The MS&L built the New Holland pier 500m long, to clear the shallows at low tide, and paddle steamers were employed to minimise the draught, but some locals believe the steamers occasionally used their paddles as wheels, to run in over the mud. In 1969 a hovercraft service was introduced: faster than the ferries when it arrived at all, it was dogged by mechanical failures and withdrawn later the same year.

New Holland pier still exists, and is still served by a rail connection, which is rarely used today. New Holland Town

New Holland Pier (above) and New Holland Town stations in 1962. (John Meredith)

station was demolished but a small halt called New Holland, just south of the connection with the Barton-upon-Humber branch, is still served by that line.

The last three ferries to serve the route have all been preserved. *Lincoln Castle* can now be seen in the docks at Grimsby; *Wingfield Castle*, built in Hartlepool, is back there as a centrepiece to the Hartlepool Historic Quay area; and *Tattershall Castle* is moored on the Embankment in London. Having a drink in one of *Tattershall Castle's* bars now is very different from doing this as she butted into the Humber in a bitter east wind!

The Lincoln Castle, *taken just before the end of the service in 1981. (Peter Grey)*

4
Into the Hills

The Horncastle branch
The Spilsby branch
Louth to Bardney

Many believe Lincolnshire is flat, but the Lincolnshire Wolds are certainly hills, and they presented problems to the railway companies that tried to build into or through them. They were surrounded by railway lines, with the ELR running up the east side, the Lincolnshire Loop and the GC line from Lincoln to Grimsby on the west and north, and the New Line crossing to the south.

Three companies eventually opened lines into the Wolds, with branches serving Horncastle and Spilsby, and the single-line link from Bardney on the Loop to Louth on the ELR.

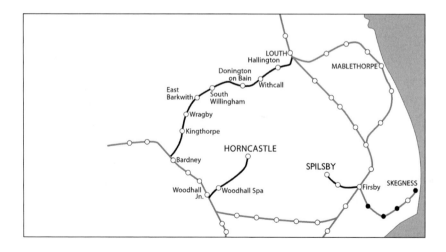

The Horncastle branch

Built by the Horncastle & Kirkstead Junction Railway Company, the seven-mile single-track line opened in 1855, linking Horncastle to the GN at Kirkstead station on the Lincolnshire Loop line.

Given that this was a fairly small railway, the celebrations in Horncastle at the opening spared no expense. Four triumphal arches were erected in the town streets, and a procession, which seems to have incorporated the whole town, visiting dignitaries and two brass bands, was led by 'a navvy bearing a pick and shovel, gilded and trimmed with flowers'. Presumably it was the tools that were decorated, rather than the navvy! The dinner for 80 local supporters featured more courses than a modern reader might credit, all with wine.

The intermediate station was to have been at Roughton, but actually became a single platform halt in the then very small village of Woodhall Spa, where rather pungent bromo-iodine mineral waters had been discovered and a hotel and spa

A railway inspector returns down the platform at Woodhall Spa station after checking the facilities.

An RCTS special arriving at Horncastle station in 1954. (Malcolm White)

constructed. Railway posters promoting the town tended to dwell more on the golf, walking and riding in the area than the waters themselves!

The spa developed rapidly, and the station was rebuilt in 1889 to include better facilities for the likes of Queen Alexandra and Princess Helena, who regularly visited the local MP, Sir Archibald Weigall, at his home in what is now the Petwood Hotel. For many years a through coach operated between Horncastle and King's Cross. It was hauled to Boston by the local train, then attached to the Grimsby–London express coming off the ELR. Ticket collectors on the return journey had to check on passengers boarding at King's Cross to ensure that they didn't end up in a small inland market town rather than at an important port.

From the beginning the line was operated by the GN, but the HKJRC retained its independence right through to the 1923 Grouping. Its principal goods traffic was agricultural produce and coal, but special trains were regularly laid on for the Horncastle Sheep and Horse Fairs, which were major events in the area. After the 1921 Sheep Fair more than 10,000 sheep were loaded at Horncastle station, and the railways themselves might have been important customers at the Horse Fair, since, just before the First World War, they owned nearly 15,000 horses to pull their local delivery carts and wagons.

At one time it was planned to extend the line through the Wolds to link up with the Spilsby branch, offering a through route to the coast, but the cost of tunnelling was too high. The line did increase the importance of Horncastle as a market centre, with carrier carts expanding their routes to the town through the second half of the nineteenth century. Excursions to Woodhall Spa were often to be seen on the branch, as were trips to Lincoln, London or the sea.

Paratroops were billeted around Woodhall Spa before the Arnhem airborne landings, and serving them, and the airfield next to the village, provided plenty of traffic for the line, although, when he visited the soldiers just before the landings, the King left his train at Woodhall Junction to complete the journey by car. The Kirkstead Home Guard made good use of

C12 tank No 69253 waits at Woodhall Junction with the Horncastle branch line set of coaches. They had been converted from two of the GNR steam railmotors. (R.K. Blencowe)

the service when set an exercise to capture the HQ of the Woodhall section. The Kirkstead men caught the train, passed through the defensive positions undetected, and captured their target without a shot being fired.

The railway was damaged by a land mine dropped by parachute in 1942. It was designed to explode above ground, and demolished the Royal Hotel and Winter Gardens, which lay alongside the track. The service was quickly restored, but the hotel and a nearby footbridge were never replaced. Ironically, the space left is now the site of the Dam Busters Memorial to the crews of 617 Squadron, based at Woodhall, who attacked the Ruhr dams in May 1943.

During the war, the line was looked after by an all-woman track gang, who walked the route checking for faults, knocking loose chair blocks back into place and keeping the ballast free of weeds. The first train of the day ran direct from Boston, crossing the goods yard at Woodhall Junction. If snow fell overnight, the gang was called at 5 am to clear the points so it could get through.

Passenger service on the branch ended in 1954, despite a vigorous local campaign, let down by the discovery that the campaigners rarely used the service. The driver of the last train to Horncastle noted the large number of passengers and commented that he would have liked to take them to Horncastle and make them walk back.

The line remained open for goods until 1971, but the years after 1954 saw a casual approach, with engine men remembering mushroom-collecting stops at the trackside, snares set for rabbits, which were collected the following day, and regular arrangements trading coal for eggs or garden produce. Crossing keepers were gone from the branch by this time, so the train

Newton Loynes, NFU Lincolnshire county secretary in 1971, was issued this special ticket and pass for the final goods train from Woodhall Junction to Horncastle in 1971. Almost certainly the last ticket to be issued to a passenger on the line.

guard had to get down to open and close all the gates. Driver Maurice Andrews admitted that he left his guard behind once while chatting to the fireman.

Most of the line from Woodhall Spa to Horncastle can easily be followed today, since it forms part of the Viking Way long-distance path. The first mile, from Woodhall Junction to Woodhall Spa, is more difficult, although some of the overgrown trackbed can be seen from Witham Road. In Woodhall it passed through what is now the car park of the Budgens store, then behind the Mall public house, although a line of bungalows has been built on it.

The trackbed crossed the road at an angle just in front of the Post Office and passed behind the shops of the Broadway. The end building – the Woodhall Wedge – tapers to a point where the line ran close behind it. The line can then be walked behind the shops and across the site of a level crossing before the path

Martin Bridge is the only overbridge on the line. The Viking Way footpath now passes under it, following the route of the railway. (Author)

leaves the original trackbed where it crosses a golf course. The stations at Woodhall Spa and Horncastle have been obliterated, with a police station at Woodhall and a tyre depot and housing at Horncastle.

The Spilsby branch

The four-and-a-half-mile line from the ELR at Firsby to Spilsby never had the financial success of its counterpart to Horncastle. The company struggled to find the money to build the line, and although it opened in 1868 it was bankrupt by 1881, and had to be taken over by the GN, which had operated it from the beginning.

There was only one intermediate station on the line, at Halton Holegate, which had a short platform, a single siding and a goods shed. Trains only stopped by request, so it probably contributed little to the financial health of the line. Seven or eight return passenger trains a day were run for much of the branch's existence, but passenger numbers were always low, even on market day, since most of the market trade came down from the hills, rather than from the coast, where shoppers could visit larger towns, such as Louth.

One market train from Skegness had a narrow escape when the locomotive coming into Firsby to couple up to it overran signals. Fortunately, the loco was diverted into a siding, where it crashed into the buffers and was derailed. No one was hurt, although the signalman had to make a fast exit from his box at the end of the siding.

There were special occasions such as the annual May Day, and limited passenger facilities at Spilsby were stretched to cater for them. Goods traffic was always the main reason for existence, with grain, potatoes and livestock leaving and coal and animal feed coming in.

One porter remarked how surprisingly often a sack of potatoes would 'accidentally' split open on cold days, allowing part of its contents to be roasted on the signal box stove. Another, who had the task of refilling the chocolate machine on

Halton Holegate station in the late 1940s. (Great Northern Railway Society)

the platform, occasionally 'dropped' a bar, which therefore could not be sold and had to be shared out, rather than be thrown away.

Sugar beet was an important seasonal commodity, although it was often a source of friction between railway staff and the farmers. If the farm cart went up onto the loading dock, the transfer into a railway wagon alongside was a relatively easy operation, but if the farmer was out of favour, the stationmaster could insist on loading with the cart kept at ground level. At one station, the stationmaster insisted on the load being tipped onto the ground and thrown up from there. Not surprisingly, that soon became another goods traffic lost to the roads.

Tallow probably came in for the soap works at Spilsby, but they closed soon after the line opened, most likely to the relief of most inhabitants – soap-boiling was a smelly business.

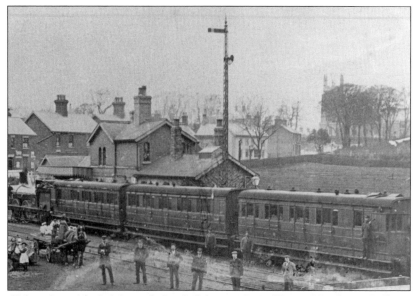

GN train with 0-4-2 tank in Spilsby station. (Great Northern Railway Society)

The Partney Sheep Fair, held a few miles away every September, was a chaotic time at Spilsby station, the railhead for the event. Several thousand sheep were moved out of the area by train, and there were lots of opportunities for confusion. Extra staff were drafted into Spilsby for the day, including the Burgh-le-Marsh horse shunter, complete with horse, who had the job of moving filled livestock wagons away from the loading dock and bringing another in to take its place.

A steam railmotor was tried on the branch in the 1930s, but even this limited capacity proved too much to support, and the line was closed to passengers shortly after the outbreak of the Second World War. Goods continued through the war and up to late 1958 when they, too, ceased and the line was lifted shortly after it had served as an overnight base for the Royal Train carrying the Duke of Edinburgh to visit an anti-aircraft rocket site near Grimsby.

Spilsby station buildings, 1954. (Great Northern Railway Society)

The line is not easy to follow today. Spilsby station is now an industrial estate, although the goods shed can still be seen, in modified form. Halton Holegate station is a private house, with the goods shed still intact behind it, but most of the track has returned to farmland, although one or two stretches can still be picked out as farm roads.

Louth to Bardney

Many railway prospectuses held wildly over-ambitious aims, but few can have gone over the top quite so comprehensively as the Louth & Lincoln Railway, which built the twenty-mile branch line from Louth to Bardney.

According to the prospectus, the line was guaranteed a profitable future, because of the amount of ironstone that could be excavated along its route, the vast expected traffic in coal for export and the large numbers of holiday-makers who would have a shorter journey to Cleethorpes and Mablethorpe. Sadly, despite the expert predictions, no ironstone was ever dug and the only coal carried was destined for local merchants along the line. The passenger traffic to the coast also never materialised after plans to join the GN at Five Mile House, with through trains running from Lincoln, had to be dropped in favour of a junction at Bardney. Would-be trippers would have had to change trains twice en route, at Bardney and Louth, rather than the through services offered by the GN and GC.

Even if the Five Mile House junction had been possible, it is unlikely that the locomotives would have been able to haul heavy goods or passenger trains over the line since the company had tried to avoid tunnelling costs by including some steep gradients over the Wolds. The route was eventually revised to reduce the gradients, but only at the cost of digging two tunnels, on either side of Donington station. The line that was eventually built was a classic country railway, wandering through

A C12 4-4-2 tank in BR livery leads the two-coach branch set out of Kingthorpe. (Peter Grey collection)

attractive countryside, and would have made an ideal candidate for preservation had it not closed long before the preservation movement took off. Of the stations only Wragby served a community of any size. Kingthorpe is so small that it is almost impossible to find nowadays, and East Barkwith, South Willingham, Donington on Bain, Withcall and Hallington are not much bigger. Delicate negotiations had to take place near Louth, where the line would have passed close by the rifle range used by the local Volunteers!

The line opened in 1876, was close to bankruptcy by 1880 and was taken over by the GN the following year, at a price less than half of what it had cost to build.

A single track, with each station having passing loops, at least one siding served by cattle pens and a loading dock, sufficed for the life of the line, with five passenger trains a day provided for the first few years, dropping to four very shortly and finally reduced to three during the Second World War. Two goods trains a day ran for most of the line's existence, but this declined to a single service by the 1950s.

East Barkwith station. (Peter Grey collection)

Although some of the gradients on the line were eased, it was still a stiff climb out of Louth for the small, and usually old, engines serving out their time on the branch. The conditions in the tunnels could be most unpleasant. One driver recalled how his fireman was almost overcome by the smoke and fumes in Withcall tunnel after the train had to back out and take a second run to get through.

During the Second World War huge numbers of bombs were brought in by train and delivered to the RAF stations on the line, or stored in ammunition dumps along the verges of the Bluestone Heath Road, an ancient highway running over the hills above Donington on Bain. The road had wide verges, and large numbers of bombs could be kept relatively safely, although locals needed special passes to travel the road because of worries about saboteurs. According to railwayman Percy Carter, one raid had to be cancelled completely when the locomotive bringing a bomb train proved too big to pass through Withcall tunnel.

On another occasion, thirteen wagons, each carrying one large bomb, ran away from South Willingham station, smashing the gates at East Barkwith, crossed the main road at Wragby (where a warning allowed the crossing keeper to open the gates) and

A C12 4-4-2 tank leaving Bardney for Louth in GN days. (Peter Grey collection)

66

Donington on Bain station then (Great Northern Railway Society) and now (Author).

appeared certain to run into the regular pick-up goods train from Bardney. Fortunately, that train was late and the runaways slowed on the rise to Kingthorpe, eventually coming to rest with no major damage done.

After the war the line suffered a major explosion when a wagon full of propane gas cylinders packed in straw caught fire. Fireman Geoff Jackson and guard Arthur Dodman uncoupled the wagons behind the burning one so it could be drawn away, then uncoupled in front of it to move the rest of the train. Both men were badly burned, with Jackson caught in the actual explosion a few seconds later. Along with driver John Ingoldmells, they received medals from the LNER for their bravery.

Closure to passengers took place on 3 November 1951, and members of the Gainsborough Model Railway Society, who joined the last train, remember it as a riotous occasion. The line was closed to goods in sections between 1956 and 1960, with the final part, from Bardney to Wragby, lost in February 1960.

Much of the route can be followed today, although it is generally in use as farm roads, so permission should be sought to wander along it. It is hardest to follow on either side of Wragby, where the line has been incorporated into fields. All the intermediate stations are intact, and most are private homes, including the well-preserved premises at Donington on Bain. Both tunnels are intact, and occasional visits have been arranged on special occasions, but the most evocative reminder of the line may be the ghost train that can be heard at Hallington station. The last reputable 'hearing' took place in 1969, but a modern visitor might be lucky.

5
Rails to the Seaside

Trains to Sutton and Mablethorpe
The New Line

Carrying holiday-makers to the seaside became an important business for many railway companies, and the successful resorts had good railway connections. Cleethorpes, Mablethorpe, Sutton on Sea and Skegness all owed their popularity to the ease with which visitors from the industrial towns and mining areas of Yorkshire and the Midlands could travel to their favourite watering places.

Cleethorpes and Skegness are still connected by rail, although the services are often inadequate to handle a holiday rush, but the lines to Mablethorpe and Sutton, and the New Line, designed to offer a short cut to the resorts, have all been lost, along with the Midland & Great Northern Joint Railway. The M&GN did not serve the Lincolnshire resorts, but did pass through the county.

Trains to Sutton and Mablethorpe

At the time that the railways were built the future resorts of Mablethorpe and Sutton on Sea were small villages of less than 350 residents, and the area was best known as summer grazing land for cattle. The original railway services were set up to develop the farming, and the first line to be built, by the Louth & East Coast Railway (L&ECR), was a thirteen-mile single track branch from Louth to Mablethorpe which opened in 1877. The company assumed that traffic would be light, and mainly agricultural, so the stations at Grimoldby, Saltfleetby and

Theddlethorpe were small and basic, and the line was laid as single track.

As industry developed, seaside visits became something for the masses, rather than the aristocrats and poets who had spent time beside the sea before the late 1870s, and the potential for passenger traffic became apparent. 'Pavilions' were erected on the foreshore at Mablethorpe, and as visitor numbers built up, its neighbour, Sutton on Sea (recently renamed from the less euphonious Sutton le Marsh), looked for its own connection to the national railway system.

It came first from a surprising direction, when the Alford & Sutton Tramway was opened in 1884 between the coast and the market town of Alford, which was already served by the ELR. The tramway was narrow gauge, laid along the road between the two towns, passing through the small villages of Bilsby, Markby and Hannah. The coaches and goods waggon – often in mixed trains – were hauled by small tram locomotives with vertical boilers, and, despite predictions of financial collapse, the

Station staff at Sutton on Sea with GN railmotor No 6. (Great Northern Railway Society – Eric Neve)

line thrived until a new seven-mile single track standard gauge line was opened in 1886, linking Sutton with Willoughby, also on the ELR.

Although the Sutton & Willoughby Railway (S&W) did provide for the seaside visitors and the local agricultural trade, it was built as part of a much bigger scheme that would have included a major dock development at Sutton. The Lancashire, Derbyshire & East Coast Railway (LD&EC) was planned to run from Warrington over the Pennines to Chesterfield and Lincoln, then on to Sutton on Sea. As with so many such schemes it failed to raise enough money, and finished just a line from Chesterfield to Lincoln; the docks were never built (see Chapter 8).

Despite the collapse of these plans, the S&W successfully established itself as a seaside and farming branch, with a single tiny station at Mumby Road between its two towns. The line was extended in 1888 to meet the Louth and East Coast at Mablethorpe, completing the loop from Louth to the coast and back to Willoughby. The whole system remained single track throughout its existence, although passing loops were provided at the stations.

Mumby Road station. (Great Northern Railway Society)

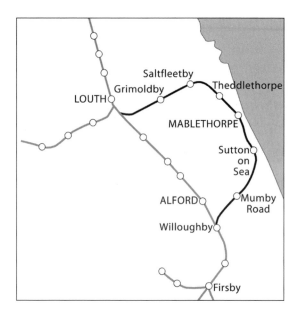

The new link crossed the tramway on the edge of Sutton, and despite the closure of the smaller line only a year later, the signal box controlling the trains remained in existence as Tramway Crossing for the rest of the railway's life. It survived the closure of the railway and sat alone in the middle of a field until, in the 1980s, it was restored as part of Mike Legge's railway museum at Legbourne Road station. The museum is now closed, but the box can be seen from the roadside.

The two local railway companies suffered financially from the failure of the LD&EC scheme, and early in the twentieth century they were taken over by the GN, which had been operating both lines for a proportion of the takings. Both then settled into the routine of holiday branches with a supporting local passenger and goods service. Over 80,000 passengers used the two lines in 1889, building to a peak of nearly 170,000 just before the Second World War. On the August Bank Holiday 1951, nineteen special trains arrived at Mablethorpe station. As with neighbouring Skegness, strong ties developed between the resorts and the

A busy day at Mablethorpe in the early days of the twentieth century. (From the Museum of Lincolnshire Life, by courtesy of Lincolnshire County Council)

mining communities of Nottinghamshire and Derbyshire, with miners' holiday and retirement homes still to be found until relatively recently.

Ironically, the link from Sutton to Mablethorpe, put in as a concession by the L&ECR, proved to be a problem for the older line. Since most of the holiday traffic approached from the south, the GN found it easier to bring excursion trains from Willoughby over the S&W rather than on the L&ECR line from Louth. Although early services on the lines tended to run from Willoughby or Louth to the sea, by the 1950s most trains ran round the whole loop. Up to a dozen trains a day served the branches, and the growth of the resorts, compared to the stagnation of earlier rivals such as Saltfleet and Frieston Shore (which had no rail links), shows the importance of the railways.

In both World Wars military traffic boosted the use of the line, with large numbers of training areas served in the First World War, and the coastal defences plus the airfields at Manby and Strubby in the Second. In both wars, to protect against invasion, many railway bridges over the fen drains were mined. At least

A picture postcard view showing LNER D2 4-4-0 4371 on an excursion train to Mablethorpe in 1927. (From the Museum of Lincolnshire Life, by courtesy of Lincolnshire County Council)

one bridge is reported to have been blown up either during an exercise or as a result of a misunderstanding, but the matter was duly 'hushed up' for security reasons.

A large naval gun had been mounted on a railway chassis to help defend against invasion, and it moved round the branches to prevent location by German aircraft. Many locals felt that it would have been of little use, since it could only fire along the direction of the line. If it had tried to shoot either side of that line, the recoil would have blown it off the tracks. One ex-artilleryman suggested that it could have done a lot of damage to Grimsby, but not much to an invading army!

During the floods of 1953, when large areas of the coast were inundated after the sea defences failed, one family is reported to have escaped the water by riding a man-powered rail trolley to safety. The track was severely damaged by the water, and both Mablethorpe and Sutton stations were flooded. To speed repairs large amounts of slag from the Scunthorpe steel works were brought by train to help rebuild the defences, which have remained secure to the present day.

The usual loss of goods traffic to the roads, and the decline in passenger numbers, particularly out of the holiday season, resulted in the Louth–Mablethorpe line closing in December 1960, along with the three village stations it served. Sadly, a Mrs Lowry, who had travelled on the first train on the line in 1877, was unable to join the final journey at Saltfleetby because of the cold weather.

Services continued between Willoughby and Mablethorpe for another ten years until the Beeching axe fell on that line as well. Local protests about the effect on tourism were countered by reminders about the losses incurred out of season and by suggestions that long-distance coaches were available from all the main visitor areas.

Saltfleetby station in 1960. (From the Local Studies Collection, Lincoln Central Library, by courtesy of Lincolnshire County Council – M. Thompson)

The final train from Mablethorpe, on 3 October 1970, was packed to the roof, with an estimated 500 people and a coffin with a party of 'mourners', accompanied by a pramful of beer, crammed into a train with just over 100 seats. The train made an unofficial stop on a level crossing in Sutton to allow the 'funeral party' to get down to continue the wake – and replenish their stock of beer – in a local hotel.

Today the lines are difficult to follow in many places. On the outskirts of Louth the track is mostly built over, although Gresley Road may have been named after the famous LNER engineer. East of the town, it has returned to farmland, although it reappears as field boundaries and a farm road as it passes through Stewton and continues towards Grimoldby. It is lost in fields west of the village, but the station is still in good condition and in use as a private house. Between Grimoldby and Saltfleetby St Peter the track can only be traced by field boundaries and hedge lines, but it is clear again through the station at Saltfleetby, which is also lived in and in good condition.

Across the farmland between Saltfleetby and Theddlethorpe the best indications are the occasional crossing keeper's cottages and the bridges across the frequent drains in the area. Ironically, those bridges, built to take the light trains of mid-Victorian times, were a problem in later years, when all locomotives had to slow to 10 mph to cross them. One of the drains also received a locomotive which was accidentally diverted into a siding rather than the main line. Theddlethorpe station is also a private house.

From Theddlethorpe to the outskirts of Mablethorpe the line is mostly obliterated, although there is a stretch as a farm road and, later, as the boundary to a large caravan site. Barely a trace remains in the resort itself, apart from the Mablethorpe station clock preserved in the reception area of the Station Sports and Leisure Centre, built on the station site.

An enthusiastic searcher could probably trace parts of the trackbed on to Sutton on Sea as access roads to a caravan site and by the alignment of various estates built along the line of track, but little else remains, and, apart from the stationmaster's house, the station is totally obliterated. South of Sutton a mile-and-a-

Two BR diesel multiple units (DMUs) in Willoughby station in the 1960s. (R.K. Blencowe)

half of trackbed has become a nature reserve and walk, and the route can also be clearly seen from the main A52 coast road until it swings away across the fields towards Mumby Road station. A substantial blue-brick road bridge remains as a traffic hazard next to the station site, where the very attractive stationmaster's house is being lived in, and the station yard and platform locations appear to be in use as industrial premises.

For about half a mile, the track is then lost into fields, but it reappears, and can be traced as a line of trees or farm tracks all the way into the station site at Willoughby. The final mile into Willoughby is another nature reserve and footpath.

The New Line

The line across the Fens from Coningsby Junction, on the GN's Lincolnshire Loop line, to Bellwater Junction on the ELR, was also a key part of the route to the sea, even though it did not

G. N. R.

OPENING OF NEW LINE
BETWEEN
KIRKSTEAD AND LITTLE STEEPING
(VIA CONINGSBY).

On **TUESDAY, 1st JULY, 1913,** the New Line between Kirkstead and Little Steeping (via Coningsby) will be opened for Passenger, Parcels, and General Merchandise traffic.

THE NEW STATIONS ARE AS FOLLOWS :—

CONINGSBY, TUMBY WOODSIDE, NEW BOLINGBROKE, STICKNEY, MIDVILLE.

The Passenger Train Service will be as shewn below :—

WEEK DAYS ONLY.

		a.m.	a.m.	a.m.	p.m.	p.m.
LONDON (King's Cross)	dep.	5 5		7 A 15	12 30	
BOSTON	„	7 57	8.35 a.m.	10 A 55	3 35	
KIRKSTEAD	arr.	8 27	from Sheffield.	11 A 18	4 6	
DONCASTER	dep.	8 9		8 42	2 10	4 47
LINCOLN	„	9 15	9 44	11 5	4 0	5 55
KIRKSTEAD	arr.	9 38	10 8	11 26	4 23	6 18
KIRKSTEAD	dep.	9 39	10 9	11 30	4 25	6 19
CONINGSBY	„	9 48	Will not run on Bank Holidays.	11 39	4 34	6 28
TUMBY WOODSIDE	„	9 56		11 47	4 42	6 36
NEW BOLINGBROKE	„	10 4		11 55	4 50	6 44
STICKNEY	„	10 12		12 3	4 58	6 52
MIDVILLE	„	10 20	D	12 11	5 6	7 0
LITTLE STEEPING	arr.			12 20		
FIRSBY	arr.	10 32		12 25	5 18	7 12
FIRSBY (for Skegness)	dep.	10 38		12 30	5 22	7 18
WAINFLEET	„				5 30	
SKEGNESS	arr.	10 53	11 7	12 45	5 39	7 34
SUTTON-ON-SEA	„	11 A 6		1 15	7 33	7 C 47
MABLETHORPE	„	11 A 13		1 25	7 40	7 C 54
BOSTON	„	11 41		1 0	6 46	7 48
LONDON (King's Cross)	„	3 55		4 45	10 45	10 45

WEEK DAYS ONLY.

		a.m.	a.m.	p.m.	p.m.	p.m.
LONDON (King's Cross)	dep.	5 E 5	10 35	12 30	4 0	
BOSTON	„	8 E 0	1 A 10	3 45	6 20	
MABLETHORPE	„		12 36	3 10	6 A 10	
SUTTON-ON-SEA	„		12 43	3 18	6 A 16	
SKEGNESS	„	8 25	1 25	4 0	6 25	8 0
WAINFLEET	„	8 35				
FIRSBY (from Skegness)	arr.		1 40	4 15	6 40	
FIRSBY	dep.		1 45	4 20	6 48	
LITTLE STEEPING	„	8 50	1 50	4 25		
MIDVILLE	„	8 59	1 59	4 34	7 0	D
STICKNEY	„	9 7	2 7	4 42	7 8	Will not run on Bank Holidays.
NEW BOLINGBROKE	„	9 15	2 15	4 50	7 16	
TUMBY WOODSIDE	„	9 23	2 23	4 58	7 24	
CONINGSBY	„	9 31	2 31	5 6	7 32	
KIRKSTEAD	arr.	9 40	2 40	5 15	7 41	8 58
KIRKSTEAD	dep.	8 42	2 43	5 18	7 43	8 59
WASHINGBORO'	„		3 1			
LINCOLN	arr.	10 7	3 10	5 43	8 8	9 25
DONCASTER	„	11 48	4 29	30	9 14	Due to arrive Sheffield 10-30 p.m.
KIRKSTEAD	dep.	9 48	4 B 16	7 10		
BOSTON	arr.	10 16	4 B 47	7 38		
LONDON (King's Cross)	„	1 5	8 15	10 45		

A. Bank Holidays excepted. **B.** On Fridays only, leaves Kirkstead 3.38 p.m. and arrives Boston 4.10 p.m. **C.** Fridays and Saturdays only. **D.** Will call at Midville on Mondays and Wednesdays when necessary to leave or take up Sheffield Passengers. **E.** Via Little Steeping.

London, King's Cross Station, June, 1913.   C. H. DENT, General Manager.

800/10,000—16-6-13.   [W. & S. Ltd.]   (32505)

78

actually run to the coast. It was opened in 1913 by the GN as a short cut for trains heading to its resorts, which, up to that time, had to take a long and roundabout route with reversals at Boston or Louth.

A direct route from Lincoln was desirable, and, having considered linking the Horncastle and Spilsby branches with a line that would have to punch through the Wolds, the GN opted to build the Kirkstead & Little Steeping Railway – universally known as 'The New Line' – across the flat fenland further south. Despite work being held up on occasion by floods, the line took only eighteen months to build, helped by the fact that it was almost level for its whole run. Brick and slate stations with quite elaborate booking halls were built at Coningsby, Tumby Woodside, New Bolingbroke, Stickney and Midville.

At the opening of the line, 130 children were marched to the station at Stickney, singing the National Anthem and waving flags. The local rector, Rev G.H. Hales, is reported to have bought the first ticket to be issued at the station, with the intention of having it framed and 'handed down for posterity'. Sadly, no record of its survival has been found.

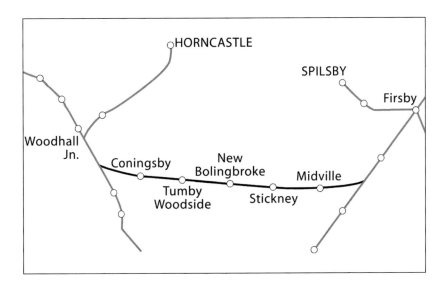

The line was laid as double track, capable of carrying heavy excursion trains, but in 1916 one of the lines was lifted and sent to the Western Front in France to help the British war effort. Unfortunately, the German navy sank the ship carrying them. The track was reinstated in time for the summer holiday season in 1923.

Initially, four trains a day ran between Lincoln and Skegness, including one through train a day to and from Sheffield. This fell to three at the 1923 Grouping, rose again to five between the wars, but was down to three again in the 1950s. The basic service was heavily supplemented by excursions and specials, with evening excursions to Skegness popular between the wars, and regular fishermen's trains to the fenland rivers and drains.

The goods service on the line was the usual local trade in coal and agricultural produce. Bombs and other munitions provided important traffic during the Second World War to the bomber bases of RAF Coningsby and East Kirkby. Stickney station might easily have disappeared on one occasion when a train of ten-ton bombs was being unloaded. The crane moving the lethal load brought down a power line which lay, sparking and flashing, over the bomb. An airman dragged the wires away, but, rather than being praised for his heroism, he was reprimanded for risking his life!

'We moved everything that moved,' commented George Houlden, who worked at Coningsby during the war. 'There was no petrol to spare for lorries, so everything went by rail, from the airmen themselves to building materials for the airfields and the big bombs for the heavy raids.' A sadder traffic was the removal of the bodies of dead aircrew whose aircraft had made it back to base. The stationmaster's young daughter made sure no coffin left without a floral tribute from the station garden.

Another story is told of a stationmaster at Tumby whose daughter left her handbag on the train. It was rescued at Stickney and sent back, but he insisted on charging her the fare for a package sent by rail!

After the war, seaside holidays and days out remained popular, but buses and the private car took their toll, and the New Line was part of the massacre of rail service in east

Tumby Woodside station then (Great Northern Railway Society) and now (Author).

Lincolnshire. Goods services went in 1964, and the line finally closed on 5 October 1970.

Following the route of the New Line today is difficult. Coningsby Junction is almost hidden in private woodland, so it is no longer possible to wait there to see if the ghost of Charlie Moody still appears. Charlie was a fireman killed when his new boots slipped on the footplate and he fell under the locomotive tender.

Parts of the embankment and river bridge at Coningsby are intact, but little now remains of the station other than the stationmaster's house and two cottages. The booking office and the house survive as private dwellings at Tumby Woodside, and recently work was going on to clear trees and undergrowth from the platforms. At New Bolingbroke the booking office houses an antique shop.

Stickney and Midville stationmasters' houses are still lived in, and the Midville booking office is intact, and used as a store, but the route of the trackbed itself can frequently be detected only by the remnants of the brick abutments of the bridges and the crossing keepers' houses, often situated out on a minor road with no apparent reason for their presence.

6

The 'Muddle and Go Nowhere'

The Midland & Great Northern Joint Railway was known to its detractors as the 'Muddle and Go Nowhere' as it served few significant towns and crossed a lot of rather empty country. The line was stitched together from smaller companies set up to serve several Norfolk seaside resorts; the farming communities of Norfolk, south Lincolnshire and Cambridgeshire; the ports of Wisbech, Spalding, King's Lynn, Blakeney, Great Yarmouth and Lowestoft; and Norwich and Peterborough.

Most of the trackwork lay outside Lincolnshire, but the main line to the Midlands ran from a junction with the Midland Railway at Saxby, crossed the GN main line at Little Bytham, then on through Bourne, Spalding, Holbeach and Sutton Bridge before crossing into Norfolk at the county boundary.

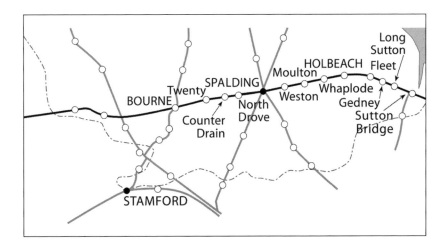

The first Lincolnshire section to be opened was built by the Norwich & Spalding Railway, an over-ambitious title, since it only applied to Parliament to build from Spalding to Sutton Bridge, and actually managed to lay a mere 7½ miles of track from Spalding to Holbeach. That opened in 1858, with intermediate stations at Weston, Moulton and Whaplode, and was worked for the next three years by the GN. A further ten-year lease started in 1861, and the line was completed through to Sutton Bridge the following year. Stations were added at Fleet, Gedney and Long Sutton.

At about the same time, the Lynn & Sutton Bridge Railway was being constructed to the east, with its costs dramatically reduced by being allowed to run trains over the Nene across the existing Cross Keys swing bridge, rather than having to build a new road and rail bridge at its own expense. That line opened in November 1864.

To the west of Spalding, the Spalding & Bourne Railway – the shorter spelling of Bourn was used in the Act – was built by the GN and opened between the two towns in 1866. A connection at Bourne with the Bourne & Essendine Railway (B&E), worked by the GN, allowed passengers and goods to continue on to the same company's main line at Essendine.

The line between Spalding and Sutton Bridge followed a slightly raised strip of land across the Fens, and ran through well-established towns and villages with a high population. By contrast, there were no significant hamlets between Spalding and Bourne, so the intermediate stations – North Drove, Counter Drain and Twenty – took their names from drainage channels across the rich fen farmland.

These lines soon fell under the control of the Midland and the GN, which operated them as the Bourne & Lynn Joint Railway. Compilers of railway quizzes have been known to set the question 'how many stations are there between Spalding and Bourne?' The answer is 'two, and Twenty'.

A short branch was added later at Sutton Bridge to serve new docks being built below the Nene bridge, which it was hoped would allow a trade in coal from the Midlands. The GN was particularly enthusiastic, investing over £50,000 in a thirteen-acre

An ex-LNER J6 0-6-0 passes the goods warehouse at Bourne. Locos of this type started my interest in the railways, since they regularly worked the line to Billingborough. (David Creasey)

dock basin with an entry lock from the tidal river, new warehouses and modern cargo-handling facilities. After the usual celebrations on completion, the *Garland*, a locally owned ship, arrived on 14 May 1881 carrying timber, which was unloaded and replaced with coal for export. Unfortunately, at this point it was discovered that the dock leaked through the silt on which its walls and lock had been built. The *Garland* and other vessels did get out, but parts of the river wall collapsed, and the dock was never used again. One stretch of the branch survived for some years to serve smaller ships coming in on the tide to deliver cargoes at a riverside wharf.

Despite this setback the Lincolnshire lines thrived, and in 1890 an extension from Bourne to join the Midland was authorised, with the support of the Norfolk companies, who had merged to form the Eastern & Midlands Railway (E&M). The new line's Act was the first document to carry the title 'Midland and Great Northern Joint Railway'. The Midland built the new link, but the

Sutton Bridge station and goods train seen from the Cross Keys bridge in the 1900s. (From the Local Studies Collection, Lincoln Central Library, by courtesy of Lincolnshire County Council)

GN added a new avoiding line to allow through trains to bypass the station at Spalding. Following financial crises, the E&M was taken over by the M&GN Joint Committee and the whole railway, from Saxby to Yarmouth formally became the M&GN in July 1893.

Goods trains were already running through from the Midlands, but a passenger service over the Saxby–Bourne stretch began early in 1894. Three stations were provided on the section, with Castle Bytham and South Witham falling inside Lincolnshire.

As usual, coal was the main incoming goods traffic, to supply the area from the Midlands coalfields. A thick bed of limestone had been exposed near Castle Bytham while building the line, and large amounts of stone were moved by rail, followed later by iron ore won by tunnelling under the limestone. Seed potatoes from Scotland were another important freight early in the year.

Agricultural produce was the most important outgoing traffic, with apples, pears, plums and soft fruit from the fenland villages between Holbeach and Sutton Bridge providing valuable trade to the company, meriting fast trains to get these to London and other cities in peak condition. Likewise the large quantities of spring flowers grown around Spalding from early in the twentieth century, which had to be carried in specially heated vans during the first few weeks of the year.

Livestock provided another seasonal trade, with stock arriving early in the spring to be fattened for slaughter on the lush grasslands near the coast during the summer. Joe Smith, a farm-worker at the time, remembered driving cattle from Gedney to Spalding for the market. There were no facilities at the market or the station for penning cattle, so if they were to be sent by train after being sold, he had to herd them himself on the street until the wagon was ready. Only then was he allowed to

Gedney station as it is now. (Author)

Loading gauge at Bourne. (David Creasey)

GN Ivatt 0-6-0 No 82 enters Holbeach station in about 1905. The station staff seem more aware of the photographer than the train. (From the Local Studies Collection, Lincoln Central Library, by courtesy of Lincolnshire County Council)

travel by train, when his sixpenny allowance provided a ha'penny bun, a penny bottle of pop and the remaining fourpence ha'penny paid his fare back home.

West of Spalding potatoes and sugar beet dominated in the autumn, but most other agricultural crops offered rail-borne trade.

The local passenger service in Lincolnshire was never very profitable – only three trains a day ran between Bourne and Saxby, although that rose to five and sometimes six a day on the more populous eastern section from Spalding to King's Lynn. Trains to Boston's Saturday market were popular, as its stalls were cheaper than the village shops. Joe mentions the 'large number of women who emerged from the station on a Saturday night, laden with baskets and parcels', and fully up to date with the latest gossip.

An excursion returns home past Bourne West box. The line curving away on the right of the picture was the branch to Essendine. (David Creasey)

A more important through-passenger business linked Midlands cities to the 'Poppyland' (north Norfolk coast) at holiday time. The best known was 'The Leicester', from that city to Yarmouth, but other fast through trains linked the beaches with Manchester, Birmingham, Nottingham, Derby and several Yorkshire destinations. However, the peak holiday season coincided with the main fruit harvest, and staff still remember the confusion when a single incident would throw the complicated timetables of through passenger trains, fast fruit specials, and local pick-up goods.

'Once it started to go, you just had to play it by ear,' one ex-signalman commented. 'I've known an excursion to go through two hours late, following three fruit specials. Fruit goes off, passengers don't!'

Despite that, the excursion business remained important well into the 1950s, but the supposed high cost of replacing the bridge over the Ouse at West Lynn, in Norfolk, triggered wholesale closure, with the line being the first main line to be closed to passengers in its entirety. That was in March 1959: one of the final trains carried a farewell headboard and the Royal Train lamp setting. Fireworks and brass bands marked the occasion and passengers packed the final trips – over 90 reportedly boarded at Bourne, rather than the usual half-dozen, and many got out at Twenty to catch the last train back. Stretches of the line, including that from Bourne to Spalding and from there on to Sutton Bridge, remained open for goods until final closure on 5 April 1965.

Trainspotters rush to get a snap of the last train on the M&GN from Spalding to Bourne in March 1959. The caption says it all. (From the Local Studies Collection, Lincoln Central Library, by courtesy of Lincolnshire County Council)

Very little of the line can now be located. Toft Tunnel, just to the west of Bourne, can be found, and is now a bat sanctuary. Bourne station ticket office is the Tudor Red Hall, originally converted for railway use by the B&E (see Chapter 7), but now serving as offices. East of the town, towards Spalding, the trackbed has been taken back as farmland, but Twenty station survives as offices. The stationmaster's house, with a railway gate, can be seen at Counter Drain, by the surviving bridges which carried the line over the Drain itself and the river Glen.

The station at Spalding is still in use, but the line itself is again difficult to follow to the east, although frequent crossing keepers' houses across fen roads show where it ran. Weston, Moulton and Whaplode stations all survive as houses, with Moulton in particular a delight, with a lawn across the trackbed, a small railway-style shelter where the opposite platform ran and the weigh office well maintained at the entrance.

At Holbeach the station and platforms were intact, but the building was unoccupied, and apparently for sale, when I

The tunnel inspection train waiting at Bourne in 1950 ready to check Toft Tunnel. (John H. Meredith)

A passenger train heading for Norfolk crosses the Cross Keys bridge in the mid-1930s. (Ralph Bates, from the Peter Grey Collection, courtesy of Lincolnshire Library service)

A sailing barge passes through the Cross Keys rail and road swing bridge at Sutton Bridge in 1907. (Great Northern Railway Society)

visited in 2007. Fleet station buildings were in excellent condition, as was the goods shed. Together they served as a house, offices and base for what appeared to be a transport company.

Gedney was in a sorry state, with the main station building still standing, but many slates off the roof and signs warning that it is in a dangerous condition. The goods shed was present until a few years ago, but has been demolished, and the same looks likely to befall the station. It, too, was apparently for sale, with some land around it, so it may become an industrial or commercial development.

The same fate appears to have already overtaken Long Sutton and Sutton Bridge stations, but the hydraulic tower at Sutton Bridge (which provided the motive power for the Cross Keys swing bridge) is still intact, with its pump house. The owners told me that the equipment could have been started up, but that the water pipes had been removed when the bridge converted to electrical operation. They had also laid a short length of track in the garden, on which stood a suburban compartment coach in Network South East livery. It will be repainted, I was assured, but negotiations were taking place between the owner, who wanted it in Southern Region green, and local friends who were keen to see the maroon BR livery carried by trains in the last years of the line.

Perhaps the finest relic of the M&GN is the Cross Keys bridge at Sutton Bridge, which replaced the original swing bridge in July 1897. The new bridge, which had carried one rail track and one road lane, was converted to allow two-way road traffic, and is still providing excellent service.

It is still worked from its fine cabin set high over the river, and is regularly swung to allow ships to pass through on their way to Wisbech. The whole operation is fascinating to watch.

7
Stamford Locals

Stamford to Essendine
Bourne to Essendine

The beautiful stone-built town of Stamford was an important stopping point on the old Great North Road from London to Edinburgh, but in the Railway Age it lost that significance to Peterborough when locals supported a cross-country line being built by the London & North Western Railway (LNWR) rather than the East Coast line of the GN. The LNWR line did not pass through Lincolnshire, other than Stamford itself, but a combination of two short lines eventually linked it to the ECML – the Stamford & Essendine, and the Bourne & Essendine.

Stamford to Essendine

The townspeople of Stamford long believed that the Marquis of Exeter was to blame for the ECML avoiding them, since he was unhappy about the line passing through the 'noble and princely and historical domain' around Burghley House. The claim has always been denied by the family; and his successor, the second Marquis, did his best to make up for the loss. He was the majority shareholder in the Stamford & Essendine Railway Company (S&E), set up in 1852 to link the town with the GN main line at Essendine, and many of the early carriages carried his personal coat of arms.

Local opposition seems to have continued: the company fell out with Stamford Corporation about land, access and Stamford police responsibility for the station, which was on the south bank of the Welland and so technically outside the town. It took

Stamford East station in its heyday (F.C. Mason, Local Studies Collection, Lincoln Central Library, by courtesy of Lincolnshire County Council) and in 1990, after conversion into sheltered accommodation (Author).

four years to construct a four-mile line, which opened in November 1856 with a single intermediate station at Ryhall & Belmesthorpe. The locals probably regretted their obstinacy when compelled to take a horse-drawn omnibus from Stamford to Tallington if they wanted to travel to London.

The Marquis insisted that the Stamford station should be built in Elizabethan style to match Burghley House. Despite some rather ugly later additions, Stamford Water Street, as it was called (to distinguish it from the earlier Midland station at Stamford Town), kept its attractive appearance throughout the existence of the line. Removal of the later excrescences means that visitors can now see it much as it was – at least from the outside! Behind the frontage the station is now a sheltered housing complex – fitting for a retired railway.

The line was built with light rail and sleepers to save money, and was operated by small 0-4-2 engines for much of its early life. In July 1878 one overshot a buffer and fell into the river. It

The Welland Diver – the locomotive that took a dip in the river. It was later recovered and put back into use. (Great Northern Railway Society)

was recovered and, once back in service, carried the unofficial title 'The Welland Diver'. Initially the line was operated by the GN, but after a dispute the S&E worked it themselves for a few years before handing back to the GN.

The key passenger services connected to the early 'Mark Lane Express', a corn merchants' train from Grantham to London, and the corresponding return service from the capital at the day's end. In the early years 'slip' coaches were detached from the train, which continued without stopping while the guard braked the coach to a stop in Essendine.

As well as coal and other materials, goods trains carried livestock to the market at Stamford. One bull decided he disliked trains, broke away from his handlers, created havoc in the station yard, then tried to swim the Welland before getting stuck in the mud and having to be rescued by railway staff. Engineering works owned by Martin's and Blackstone's also provided goods traffic, and a major military staging area nearby generated much military traffic. One tank being delivered slipped from its wagon, fortunately not on the river side!

The engine shed at Stamford East, seen from a passing train in 1956. C12 No 67398 waits to take its turn with the train. (R.K. Blencowe)

The line closed completely in June 1959, and, apart from the frontage at Stamford, little remains. The buildings at Ryhall & Belmesthorpe have gone and the trackbed is mostly in private hands, although it can be seen from the Ryhall–Stamford road and where roads cross the trackbed.

Two other lines connected with the S&E: one is described in the next section, and the other was an extension of the original company. It was planned to give Stamford a better link with the railway system at Peterborough, but the line eventually petered out at a station at Wansford Road, outside Lincolnshire.

It will never properly be known whether Stamford would have benefited from being on the GN main line. While in 1851 both Stamford and Peterborough, which is on the line, had populations of about 9,000, Stamford added fewer than 500 over the next half-century, while Peterborough grew by more than 20,000. Stamford might have grown and changed beyond all recognition. You win some; you lose some.

Bourne to Essendine

This line, from the main line at Essendine to the market town of Bourne, gave the opportunity for passengers to travel between Bourne and Stamford, or change trains at Essendine for London or the North. Like the S&E, it was supported by the Marquis of Exeter. The Bourne & Essendine Railway (B&E) had hoped to bring their line in from north of Essendine to allow a through service between Bourne and Stamford, but a local vicar objected to the damage to a favourite plantation of yews and blocked the plans.

The B&E served two stations: Thurlby and Braceborough Spa, and a halt at Wilsthorpe on the six-and-a-half mile line. Thurlby was a substantial village, and the station lay on its west edge, but the station at Braceborough was over a mile from the small village down a narrow lane. Mineral springs had been discovered nearby, and it was hoped that a spa would develop there. Spa water was sent from the station in churns. Wilsthorpe

The train for Bourne waits at Essendine station in 1951. The locomotive is a new BR Standard 2-6-0, but the coaches still carry their LNER insignia. (John H. Meredith)

itself was a mile from its halt, which was also about a mile from another hamlet at Mansthorpe.

At Bourne, the cost of a station building was substantially reduced, as mentioned in Chapter 6, by taking over an empty Tudor house – the Red Hall. The building also served as a church for the navvies building the line, which may have helped keep the line remarkably free of the disputes and disturbances which usually followed the arrival of such hard-drinking men.

Bourne had substantial goods facilities to serve the needs of an important market town and the railhead for a productive agricultural area. The weight of traffic carried is illustrated by the heavily loaded goods train heading into Bourne from Essendine which failed to stop and had to be diverted onto the Sleaford branch to allow it to run off its momentum. Another time a petrol-powered platelayer's trolley escaped from its gang near Thurlby, but stopped again just before Bourne.

Thurlby also had a goods shed and sidings, but, apart from the strong trade in potatoes and sugar beet during winter, neither of the other stops handled significant goods traffic. A siding was installed at Wilsthorpe to receive coal for the Peterborough Corporation waterworks close by, though the trade ceased when electric pumps were installed.

As with the S&E, the main passenger traffic was that connecting with the main line, although small numbers of workers and schoolchildren used certain trains during the day. The rolling stock was basic – a converted two-coach set made up from a pair of de-motored steam railcars, although even these looked luxurious compared to the cattle trucks that turned up at Thurlby once after the driver had failed to couple up the coaches to the end of his mixed train.

Sadly, passenger numbers fell to an average of five per trip in the late 1940s, and in 1947 the loss of a train for several days in

Thurlby station in GN days – before 1923. (David Creasey)

B&E train passing Carlby bridge. (David Creasey)

a snowdrift lessened the value of claims that 'the trains can always get through'. The line was closed to both passengers and goods in June 1951 and is now quite difficult to locate. The station at Bourne was demolished shortly after closure, although a fine warehouse remained for many years (now gone).

Thurlby station is now part of a local authority depot and that at Braceborough is an attractive private house with a very suitable painting of a passing train on its garage door. The crossing keeper's house can still be found at Wilsthorpe Halt, but most of the trackbed has been incorporated into farmland or farm roads. With a good OS map the crossing points can be found, but not much is accessible even to the determined walker.

8
Over the Trent

*The Lancashire, Derbyshire &
East Coast Railway
The Manchester, Sheffield &
Lincolnshire Railway*

In addition to its dominant role in north Lincolnshire, the GC also played a major part in developing the railways around Lincoln. Its line from the city to Grimsby remains in use, but the two that came in from the west have both been lost.

The LD&EC

The Lancashire, Derbyshire & East Coast Railway was another company with ambitious plans. It did not start in Lancashire, and never reached the East Coast.

The original scheme, as passed by Parliament, was the largest single railway proposal to be carried. Originally planned as a 170-mile main line to link with a new port at Sutton on Sea – referred to in Chapter 5 – it was intended to carry manufactured goods from the North and coal from Derbyshire for export. Investment in this scheme was slow, as many potential backers had had their fingers burned by railway failures, and it became apparent that it would not be possible. The LD&EC chairman declared that, although the line 'had been of world-wide importance, it had not met with world-wide subscriptions'.

The section that did get constructed was the last railway to be built to Lincoln, and opened in 1896. It ran from Chesterfield to Pyewipe Junction on the joint line just west of Lincoln, although trains were permitted to run into the city over the GN&GE Joint line under the terms of its Parliamentary bill. Such statutory access was known as having running powers.

Pyewipe Junction was so named for its proximity to the old Pyewipe Inn on the banks of the Fossdyke Navigation, another waterway taken over and controlled by the GN. The tank engines which handled much of the LD&EC's traffic were coaled and watered here. The company kept an employee permanently stationed there to do this, while the engine crew crossed the Navigation by a hand ferry to take refreshment in the pub. The line entered Lincolnshire by the massive Fledborough viaduct over the river Trent, claimed to consist of nine million bricks, and had stations at Clifton upon Trent (in Nottinghamshire), Doddington, Harby and Skellingthorpe. A couple of sidings were also provided for goods traffic.

Fledborough viaduct, looking east. (Author)

Despite the failure of the overall scheme, the railway did carry large amounts of coal into Lincolnshire, where it moved onto the GN&GE Joint for transport to the South or the GC through to the Humber ports, which built up a substantial business in export coal. From an initial four trains a day, within a decade goods traffic grew to seventy-five trains each way, a remarkable figure in view of the fact that much of it was through connections to other lines, several of which were direct competitors.

The sidings at Pyewipe Junction were bombed during the First World War, the day after the Royal Train had been stabled there, but since the Zeppelins were notorious for not knowing where they were, or what they had bombed, this is unlikely to have been planned.

The LD&EC had ambitions to become an important passenger railway, on the basis of potential excursion traffic to 'the Dukeries' in north Nottinghamshire (so-called because of the many stately homes in its attractive countryside). Browsing round stately homes was rarely possible then, although their

A coal train from the Midlands passes the site of Skellingthorpe station in the 1970s. (Peter Grey)

parks might be visited as part of an organised tour. The railway company set about organising such tours, and went so far as to build a large interchange station at Tuxford, where their line crossed the GN main line, but passenger numbers were small since few GN trains stopped there. The Dukeries Line, as it promoted itself, did attract excursions, but business must have been hindered by local aristocratic landowners' refusal to allow trains to run on Sundays, and a reluctance to permit some excursions over the line since they would have disrupted the flow of goods trains.

Local traffic would have been limited, since only four trains a day each way ran on the Lincolnshire end of the line in the early years, with one extra on Sundays, a level that did not change significantly through most the line's existence, falling to three in

The old weighhouse at Skellingthorpe has been turned into the village heritage centre. (Author)

the final years. Little attention was paid to local passenger comfort in the early years, as shown by the LD&EC purchasing second-hand Great Eastern suburban carriages, not renowned for their comfort or riding ability!

The company was taken over by the GC in 1907, became part of the LNER in 1923 and was nationalised with the rest of the railway system in 1947. Each change, perhaps inevitably, saw a reduction in traffic on the line as the owners rationalised service among the routes they owned. Passenger traffic between the stations on the line ended in 1955 and the stations were closed to goods a year later. Occasional through passenger trains carrying excursions to the coast continued for a few more years, with a final railtour special going through in September 1979.

By the 1960s goods train numbers were down to about 80 a week, reducing to a mere handful by 1980. In July 1980, when an accident damaged the track near Clifton upon Trent station, the Lincolnshire end of the line was immediately closed rather than spend money on repairs, and it was lifted the following year. West of the Trent, the line continued to supply coal to the power station at High Marnham until that closed recently.

The entire trackbed west of Lincoln is now in the hands of the cycling charity, Sustrans, and can be walked with ease, although the only remains of the sole Lincolnshire station at Skellingthorpe are the station house, with a couple of cottages, and the weigh office at the yard entrance This has been very attractively converted into a display area for Skellingthorpe Heritage, but, sadly for a railway enthusiast, the 'heritage' concentrates on the Second World War airfield nearby.

Part of a cattle dock can be found at Doddington siding, and the station house is a private residence at Doddington and at Harby stations. If you walk as far as Clifton upon Trent, you will find the station house and some of the buildings in good use. Fledborough viaduct is substantially intact, and I am told by Sustrans that their plans include extending the cycle path across the Trent on it.

Several sleeper-built seats can be found along the completed part of the cycle path, but users should be warned of the painful consequences of a creosoted splinter. I write from experience.

The loading dock at Doddington siding now. (Author)

The MS&L

The Manchester, Sheffield & Lincolnshire built its line from Clarborough Junction, close to Retford in north Nottingham-shire, to Sykes Junction, on the GN Lincoln–Gainsborough line, on the basis of plans approved by the Sheffield & Lincolnshire Junction Railway, which became part of the MS&L in 1846.

Like the LD&EC, the line entered the county over a major bridge across the Trent: the Torksey viaduct. It passed through a single station, at Torksey, and running powers over the GN allowed it to connect with the MS&L's line from Lincoln to Grimsby.

The Leverton branch, as it became known, was ready to open in January 1850, but no trains ran for six months because of the ongoing feud between the MS&L and the GN referred to in Chapter 2. The GN refused to let the MS&L over its lines to Lincoln in retaliation for its rival's tactics at Grimsby and New Holland. Even when the GN's need for access to MS&L lines at

A train picks its way through floods on the approach to Torksey viaduct in 1932. (Courtesy of Nottinghamshire County Council and www.picturethepast.org.uk)

Gainsborough forced it to cooperate, there were still arguments about watering locomotives at Retford.

Once open, in August 1850, the line served as a fast link between Sheffield and Lincoln, with nine trains a day each way on the 1922 timetable, rising to fifteen by the late 1930s. The line also carried a large number of specials, including excursions to the coast and regular fishermen's trains from Sheffield. Fishermen from the city still represent the majority along our stretch of the Witham, although the trains stopped running nearly 40 years ago.

Another group of passengers was golfers visiting the nationally known Lincoln Golf Club course alongside the station at Torksey. Golfers tempted to stay too long in the bar were warned by a bell which was rung there five minutes before the scheduled departure time of a train. It is reported that some still failed to make it, despite leaving at the bell!

Coal was, once again, the main goods commodity, from South Yorkshire pits. The few stations each served nothing more than a village, so local needs were usually met by the pick-up goods trains which ambled along the line between the through trains. By the 1950s it was apparent that the sole merit of the line, a slight reduction in transit time between Sheffield, Retford and Lincoln, did not justify the costs of keeping it open. The services were diverted along the original S&LJ Retford–Gainsborough route and into Lincoln via the Joint line, and the Leverton branch was closed in November 1959.

Ironically, two new goods flows resulted in most of the line reopening. The line west of the Trent was reinstated in 1968, to carry merry-go-round coal trains from the Yorkshire pits to a new power station at Cottam, while east of the river a wartime petroleum depot at Torksey switched to rail delivery, and the line from Sykes Junction was restored, with additional sidings

Torksey station in 1953. (From the Local Studies Collection, Lincoln Central Library, by courtesy of Lincolnshire County Council – M. Thompson)

Torksey viaduct. (Author)

feeding into the depot. The power station is still linked to the rail network, but the oil traffic ceased in 1988, and the track was lifted shortly afterwards. I was living only a mile away from Torksey at the time, and often walked on the trackbed with my dog. I expect it would be possible to walk along the line now, although some appears to be in use by local farmers. From Torksey station, now inaccessible due to a substantial house building project, it crosses a number of fields and one level crossing in the couple of miles to Sykes Junction.

9

Light Lines by the Trent

The Axholme Joint Railway
The North Lindsey Light Railway

Two railways systems were built in what is now North Lincolnshire under the Light Railways Act 1896, which allowed lines to be built to a lower engineering standard, providing light trains were run at low speeds – 25 mph on straight track and 8 mph on bends!

The lines were the Axholme Joint Railway, west of the Trent, and the North Lindsey Light Railway, to its east.

The Axholme Joint Railway

The Isle of Axholme, and adjacent Yorkshire Marshland, were cut off on three sides by rivers and on the fourth by marsh and bogs. Reclaimed in the late seventeenth century, they provide fine agricultural land, growing speciality vegetable crops as well as the usual grain, potatoes and forage crops.

Two lines still cross the Isle, the old GN&GE Joint line and the GC from Doncaster to Scunthorpe and Grimsby, but the local economy was mostly served by the Axholme Joint Railway (AJR), a combination of two local companies. The Goole & Marshland Light Railway and the Isle of Axholme Light Railway were established just before the end of the nineteenth century, but were both taken over within three years by the North Eastern and Lancashire & Yorkshire (L&Y) Railways, who combined them, in 1902, into the Axholme Joint.

As originally planned, the G&MLR would have run from a junction with the North Eastern at Marshland Junction (between

112

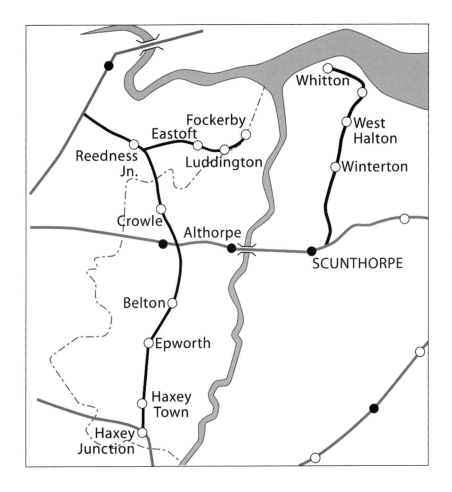

Doncaster and Goole) to Eastoft, later extended to Luddington and Fockerby. Powers were granted to continue to Adlingfleet, but the line was never extended that far. From Reedness Junction on that line, the IALR track ran south through Crowle, Belton and Epworth, the 'capital' of the Isle, to the large village of Haxey. The line was extended to the GN&GE station of the same name, with exchange facilities established at their own station, Haxey Junction, alongside the older one.

113

The bridges and embankments carrying the AJR over the South Yorkshire Navigation and the Doncaster–Scunthorpe line. (From the Local Studies Collection, Lincoln Central Library, by courtesy of Lincolnshire County Council)

In theory, passengers could change at Crowle to Crowle Central on the Scunthorpe–Doncaster line. However Crowle Central is a mile-and-a-half from the IALR station, so a traveller on foot would need to allow plenty of time to get between them. The owner of the White Hart hotel in the town did supply a horse-drawn bus, which conveyed up to ten passengers at a fare of twopence for adults and a penny for children.

A branch was built to Hatfield Moor to link with the large peat workings there, but others to Newlands and Black Carr never materialised. The line was remarkable for the sheer number of private sidings – seventeen in all, in addition to the goods facilities at the nine stations.

The two larger companies might have hoped to get into the South Yorkshire coalfield, using a projected Haxey–Tickhill link, but they built their own direct line, and the Tickhill project fell under the control of the GN. Another scheme was a tunnel under the Trent to link up with the North Lindsey Light Railway and perhaps thereby gain access to Grimsby and Immingham along the north Lincolnshire coast, but a long tunnel under a major river was never likely to be affordable by the local lines.

Some major engineering works were carried out, including the Crowle Swing Bridge over the Stainforth and Keadby Canal, a 50-ft truss girder over the Doncaster–Scunthorpe railway and two brick viaducts, one of twelve arches and one of nine.

Passenger trains were hauled at first by old L&Y engines. The LMS, which took over the line after the 1923 Grouping, used a Sentinel steam railcar, which shuttled from Goole to Haxey Junction up to five times a day and served until the end of regular passenger traffic in July 1933. The service was always slow; one gentleman I spoke to claimed he could always beat it on his bike. Also, first-class carriages were never provided on the AJR.

Goods receipts from the lines have been estimated at four times those of the passenger traffic, although Methodist excursions to Epworth, the home of the Wesleys, boosted the latter from time to time. The main income came from agricultural produce, mainly potatoes, sugar beet, peas, celery and other vegetables, as well as large amounts of peat extracted from the moors or wastes.

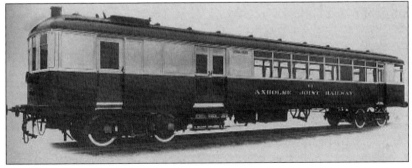

An AJR railcar.

The lines remained open to goods traffic into the 1950s, but the section from Haxey Junction to Epworth closed completely at the end of January 1956. The rest of the line was lost post-Beeching in April 1965, shortly after a railtour organised by a local school had taken a DMU along those parts still accessible.

As with most lines that crossed good agricultural land, much of the northern part of the AJR has gone back under the plough or become farm roads, although all the station houses on the Fockerby branch are lived in and the isolated Reedness Junction is clearly visible to anyone with access to the Google Earth website.

The platform building at Eastoft is still in place, and that at Fockerby appears still to be there, although it is so buried in undergrowth as to be almost impossible to identify. Luddington station house can be seen across the fields, but it lies at the end of a private road, so the state of the platform buildings could not be ascertained.

Further south, the route can be traced more easily. The swing bridge at Crowle is long gone, and the larger viaduct was demolished to ease road congestion, but the smaller nine-arch structure is still there. Crowle station house, which incorporated the booking office, is a private house.

Belton station house was still in existence in spring 2007, but it was not occupied, and much of the back had been demolished. The platform building is largely intact, but is in the garden of a neighbouring house.

A footpath runs along the trackbed between Belton and Epworth with a picnic site at the beginning of the deep cutting and short tunnel that led to Epworth. The low embankments of the goods-only Hatfield Moor branch can be seen curving in from the west to meet the main line here.

Epworth station is now an industrial estate and, although I am told the stationmaster's house is still there, I was not able to find it. A length of embankment south of Epworth does not appear to be accessible, but a bridle path and nature reserve occupy much of the rest of the trackbed to Haxey. This section can be seen from the A161 between Low Burnham and Haxey.

The station house at Haxey has a fine railway lamp-post in its front garden. South of Haxey, the line can be seen again, but is

The Hatfield Moor branch leaving the main AJR line. (Author)

less accessible. The curve into Haxey Junction can be seen, and some of the shared facilities at the station are still intact, but the area is not open to the public.

The North Lindsey Light Railway

The NLLR was the idea of the iron-making companies in Scunthorpe, who were developing new ore deposits north of the town. They saw the possibility of easier access to markets in northern England and overseas by linking into the water-borne trade on the Humber.

The line was built by the GC and ran for eleven miles to Whitton, a long-established ferry dock, with a pier used by packet boats on the river. The line also served a small port at Winteringham Haven, from where a ferry ran to Hull.

117

The first section, through Winterton & Thealby to West Halton, opened in late 1906. It was extended to Winteringham and Winteringham Haven the next summer, and completed, by the line from Winteringham to Whitton, in December 1910. If the AJR tunnel under the Trent had been built, it would have connected Whitton to Alkborough.

Initially three passenger trains ran each day, but by 1922 there were just two, one terminating at Winteringham, the other at Whitton. Since the latter arrived in the town at 1.55 pm, and left again at 2 pm, it could only have been of use for travellers needing to stay overnight. The LNER took over the line in 1923, and closed the passenger service completely two years later.

After the Second World War, life was very quiet along most of the line. The daily goods train, which carried little other than coal, left Scunthorpe at 9 am in 1948, and travelled to Whitton, where it spent four-and-a-half hours before returning. However, the southern part of the line remained busy with iron ore from the quarry lines serving the Normanby Park Ironworks, built

The first train into Winterton & Thealby station in 1906. (Photograph courtesy of North East Lincolnshire Council Library Service)

The first train into Winteringham station in June 1907. (Photograph courtesy of North East Lincolnshire Council Library Service)

alongside the line in 1912. A line also served the Trentside port of Flixborough, devastated by the explosion at the Nypro works in 1974.

Formal closure came about – like the opening – in stages. The line north of West Halton was closed in 1951, The station itself was closed ten years later, followed by Winterton & Thealby in 1964. Any possibility of a later reopening was lost when a new quarry was dug across the route at Thealby. The remainder of the line was transferred to the British Steel Corporation, which used parts of it for ore until the early 1980s. BSC's successors continue to use the Flixborough branch, as it is now known, to send steel for export through the rebuilt facilities at the port.

South of the Thealby quarry, the line can still be seen, and track was in place on it until recently. North of the quarry, parts of the route can be traced, but most has either been incorporated into farmland or built over around Winteringham. The station

Two British Steel tank engines haul iron ore over the NLLR to Scunthorpe. (Photograph courtesy of North East Lincolnshire Council Library Service)

there is still standing, converted into a house, and some remains of the trackbed can be detected along the road leading to the Haven.

North and east of Booth Nooking Lane the main line trackbed is in use as a farm road, but it disappears into the fields towards Whitton, where the station site can be found by Station Road. The station itself has been demolished, and very little trace remains.

10
Blocking the Great Eastern

Lincoln to Grantham
Sleaford to Bourne

To a large extent, the GC and the GN had Lincolnshire sewn up between them, with just a little competition from the Midland on its line to Lincoln.

Both companies carried large amounts of coal from the South Yorkshire coalfields. The GC took it to Immingham for export and the GN to London. The Great Eastern saw that it was losing out by not having a link into the coalfields, and proposed a number of lines up from its territory in Norfolk and Cambridgeshire, through Lincolnshire, into Yorkshire.

The GN saw such moves as a threat, and tried to block the GE by building lines between communities that the GE hoped to link. The battle was eventually lost by the GN, who had to agree to the construction of a joint line through the county, the main job of which would be to move coal and other freight. Most of that line is still with us, but before admitting defeat the GN built two north–south lines in the county – from Lincoln to Grantham and from Sleaford to Bourne.

Lincoln to Grantham – the line we didn't have to lose

The Grantham–Lincoln line should still be with us. The Beeching Report recommended that it should be retained as Lincoln's link to the ECML, and an alternative when that line needed to be closed for maintenance. It suggested that the line to Newark – the first railway in the county – should be closed, but

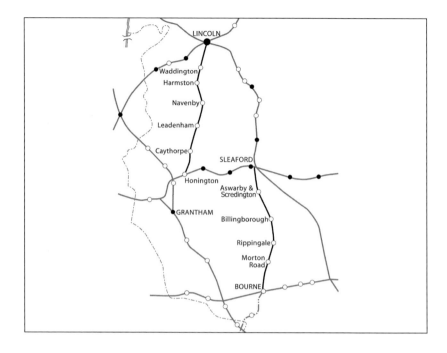

the powers-that-be rejected the proposal, kept the Newark line and closed the route to Grantham.

The eighteen-mile line had been built by local contractors Kirk and Parry of Sleaford, who began construction early in 1865 intending to have it completed within a year at a cost of just over £100,000. It actually took just over two years and the cost rose to over £120,000 before it could be opened in April 1867, with the usual fanfare and feasting. On 15 April, 300 guests dined in the goods shed at Caythorpe.

The tracks ran from the GN station in Lincoln to Honington Junction, where it joined the Grantham–Sleaford line. The junction faced Grantham, and a curve was proposed to allow trains to go east to Sleaford instead, but there is doubt as to whether this was ever built, or was built and soon lifted again.

Five stations were built on the line, at Waddington, Harmston, Navenby, Leadenham and Caythorpe, with the existing station

Caythorpe station. (From the Local Studies Collection, Lincoln Central Library, by courtesy of Lincolnshire County Council – M. Thompson)

at Honington rebuilt on the opposite side of a level crossing to serve both lines at the junction. With the line running along the edge of the Lincolnshire limestone ridge, most of the stations were some distance from the villages they served; only Leadenham was actually in the village itself.

The stations were all built to a similar plan, although a local landowner demanded that 'his' station should match the rest of the village, so Leadenham was built of stone, rather than red brick. History does not record how he felt about the company building the goods shed of brick, but since the parish boundary passed between the station and the shed, there was little he could do about it.

Leadenham has an additional claim to fame, in that the Royal Train was often stabled there during visits to the county. It was convenient for visits to the Royal Air Force College at Cranwell, and had a long siding, shaded by trees, which may have provided cover from German aircraft during the Second World War.

123

Leadenham station. (Great Northern Railway Society)

The building of the line revealed one of its most valuable freights, when it was realised that the ironstone beds alongside the track could be quarried and transported to Yorkshire and the Midlands. At the peak of the trade in the early twentieth century, up to nine quarries were worked, but that fell to one just before the Second World War and, although demand increased during the war, the last wagons of ore were filled in 1946.

Another major goods trade on the line was the delivery of coal to the Lincoln Corporation gasworks at Bracebridge, built alongside the line to ensure easy access to the large amounts needed. Coal would also have been required for the brickworks a little further along the line.

In addition to the normal passenger service of up to twelve trains a day at peak services, the line also carried trains diverted from the ECML during maintenance and upgrading, offering the local trainspotters the chance to 'cop' main-line locomotives not normally seen in the area.

A4 Dwight D Eisenhower *leaving Waddington station at the head of an express to London. The locomotive is now preserved in the National Railroad Museum of the USA. (Ralph Bates, from the Peter Grey Collection, courtesy of Lincolnshire Library Services)*

The decline began in the usual way, with all the stations except Leadenham losing their passenger and parcels service in 1962. Harmston closed completely, but the others kept their goods facilities until mid-1964 when, after the Beeching Report, all the goods yards closed. The final blow fell in 1965, when the Beeching recommendation to keep the line open was overturned, and, despite the usual campaigns, through services on the line ended on 30 October that year.

The section from Lincoln into the gasworks remained in use for a further five years, before the coming of North Sea gas ended the need for coal supplies to the works. The final parts of the track were lifted in January 1971.

Steam locomotives heading to Doncaster for scrapping pass Navenby station. (Les Camm)

If Kesteven County Council had been more supportive, it would have been very easy to follow large parts of the route, since there was a proposal before the Council to buy the seven-mile stretch from Carlton Scroop to Wellingore as a country park, but the £4,500 purchase price proved too much for a majority of the councillors and the project was dropped.

Parts of the old trackbed can still be traced in cuttings round the edge of Lincoln South Common, although it is often inaccessible through flooding. New developments and garden encroachments have made the line hard to follow from there to the old station site in Waddington. The station itself has been demolished, but the line of the track can be detected across to Somerton Gate Lane, where a level crossing hump can still be negotiated, although the crossing keeper's house has long gone. South of the crossing, the line has been incorporated into a field, but it reappears as farm tracks for much of the way to Harmston station, now used by a transport firm.

Between Harmston and Navenby the route is mostly visible, either as a track or overgrown. Navenby station is a private residence, as is Leadenham, although the brick goods shed is the base for Househam's agricultural sprayer manufacture. Between the two, the trackbed can again often be detected, although some has been incorporated into fields. A three-quarter-mile stretch along an embankment near Welbourn is waymarked as part of The Railway Walk.

A small embankment close to the entrance to the Sir William Robertson School is one of the few remaining signs of the ironstone workings, which were mostly back-filled and returned to agricultural use. The concave curve of some of the farmland running up to the hillside on the west is a result of the work.

The cuttings south of Leadenham are still visible, although the new A17 bypass crosses them close to Fulbeck, and has blocked the line.

Leadenham today. (Author)

At Caythorpe a recycling firm has taken over the station yard. The line south is often inaccessible, and has been incorporated into farmland at several points. The bridge carrying the A607 is obviously a railway bridge, but no sign of a line can be seen on either side. It reappears behind Normanton and Carlton Scroop, passing under the A607 again before curving across the fields to meet the existing line just to the east of the old Honington station site.

Sleaford to Bourne

The GN effectively admitted that it had only proposed building this line as a tactical move when it tried to drop the plan once the GN&GE Joint line was agreed, but local pressure forced them to continue. The two towns were joined in January 1872 by a sixteen-mile single-line branch that also served the villages of Aswarby, Scredington, Horbling, Billingborough, Rippingale and Morton.

Passenger numbers were never exciting, with five trains a day providing the service, at an average speed end-to-end of about 20 mph. My father can remember travelling on the train from Billingborough to the market at Sleaford, but he commented that he only did so when no other option was available – a horse and trap was often quicker and usually more comfortable! An extra train did run on Mondays, which was market day in Sleaford, but that did not increase the traffic to a commercial level, and the line was closed to passengers in September 1930.

Two specials did run from stations on the line in the early 1950s. As a child in Billingborough, I was desperate to go on the 1951 outing to the Festival of Britain! Sadly, I didn't get to go, and the later alternative of a visit to Liverpool to see the new cathedral just didn't have the same impact, although I did enjoy a ride on the 'Docker's Umbrella' (the Liverpool Overhead Railway).

Goods traffic on the line was the usual Lincolnshire mix of coal, building materials, agricultural products and farmers' supplies, although a large part of the business of the line was

The author's grandfather, on left, at Billingborough station with a dray decorated for the Jubilee of King George V. Note the GN wagon – the GN had ceased to exist twelve years earlier, but the livery had not been changed.

probably conducted in the few hundred yards from Sleaford station to the massive Bass maltings built alongside it. The Stow Green Horse Fair boosted the service to Billingborough for a few days each year, but the Fair declined rapidly after the First World War, and is no longer held, despite occasional efforts in the 1950s and 1960s to restart it (and justify all-day pub opening).

Railway tracks can still be seen set into the roadways at the old Bass maltings at Sleaford. (Author)

The goods service continued through the Second World War and after, and the occasional glimpse of an 0-6-0 goods loco with the – very short! – daily train was my first experience of railways. Goods traffic between Sleaford and Billingborough ended in July 1956, after which this part of the line was used for storing redundant wagons, although occasionally the Royal Train spent a peaceful night there. Until 1964, potatoes, grain and other agricultural produce continued to use what, following the closure of most of the M&GN, had become a dead-end branch from Spalding through Bourne to Billingborough, with the branch finally closing in 1965.

Rippingale station then (Great Northern Railway Society) and now (Author).

The old trackbed can still be identified for much of the route, although most of it is now in private ownership. Aswarby & Scredington station is in use as a private home, with light industry in the old goods shed, and Billingborough is the headquarters of Grimer's transport business, where one of the highlights of the village Christmas decorations is a train in lights puffing away on the platform.

Rippingale is a gem. It still carries the old blue and white enamel station name board, and sympathetic modifications have resulted in an extremely attractive house. Track has been relaid alongside the platform, with more planned for the yard. At the time of my visit two locomotives were stored in the yard, with items of rolling stock from the ironstone lines and other railway equipment ready for use.

Morton Road station has been incorporated into a new development, which has retained its appearance from the approach road, but been substantially modified and extended on the platform side.

11
Other Lost Lines

The Edenham branch
Potato railways
RAF Cranwell
The Lincoln Avoiding Line
Spalding to March
St Mark's station, Lincoln

The Edenham branch –
Lord Willoughby's Railway

Lord Willoughby d'Eresby was a great enthusiast for new ideas. In the middle years of the nineteenth century he experimented with steam ploughing; installed a piped water and sewerage system in his home, Grimsthorpe Castle; used portable steam engines in his sawmill and brick yards; experimented with steam road traction; and built himself a railway.

His Lordship realised that the opening of the GN's Towns Line through Grantham would improve communication with his Lincolnshire estates, and decided to build a branch from the GN station at Little Bytham to 'his' village of Edenham. A station was built at Edenham with a passenger platform, a goods shed and coal drops, and an engine shed. A single-line track was laid to Little Bytham, with exchange facilities to the GN, and the experimental road traction engine Ophir was converted into a railway locomotive.

The line was completed in 1856, with approval for passengers acquired the following year. The service took twenty minutes to cover the five-mile line, although the distance was completed in

133

Great Northern Atlantic at speed on the East Coast Main Line. (From the Local Studies Collection, Lincoln Central Library, by courtesy of Lincolnshire County Council)

just nine minutes on one occasion when his Lordship's son told the driver to disregard the speed limit so he could catch a train at Little Bytham.

The little railway did well for some years, bringing in coal for the estate and for Bourne and carrying away livestock, grain and other farm produce. The line was improved over time, to smooth out some of the sharp curves and reduce the steeper gradients, but lost traffic to the new Bourne & Saxby Railway, later part of

134

the M&GN, and is believed to have closed in 1873 after the last locomotive was sold, although it may have been worked for a while by horse haulage.

Any track that could be retrieved was sold at auction in 1890, along with any other assets of the railway that could be found. The route still exists as farm and estate roads over much of its length, and remnants of the Edenham station buildings can still be seen at Copy Lawn Farm in the village, but they have been substantially altered to fit their new use.

Potato railways

Lincolnshire is a major potato-growing area. Many of the fenland soils get waterlogged in the autumn lifting season. One solution was to lay temporary railway tracks across fields and into farmyards, and the availability of rail and equipment when the trench railways were lifted after the First World War allowed some quite substantial systems to be developed.

In his book on the subject, Stewart Squires identifies at least 34 such railways, but the two major systems were those on the

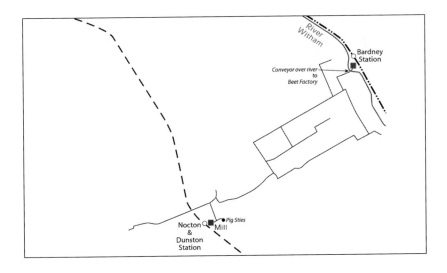

Nocton Estate, just south of Lincoln, and the Fleet Light Railway (FLR), near Holbeach.

The Nocton Potato Railway was established in 1919, but a large purchase of ex-army equipment in 1926 allowed it to extend to over twenty miles in length, with much in use all year round. From a base alongside the GN&GE Joint Nocton & Dunston station, the line ran the length of the farm, extending to the banks of the river Witham to the east and up onto the Lincolnshire Heath to the west.

A mill, workshop and potato chitting houses were served by the lines, as were the piggeries, where track was laid between the pens to allow mucking out by rail, also a quarry, a pumping engine and a gantry to carry sugar beet to a factory across the Witham. Drinking water was transported by rail to all the farmhouses and cattle sheds distributed around the estate. A fuel train of tank wagons travelled round the farm filling up individual bowsers for each of the tractors at work.

A loaded train coming back from the potato fields on the Nocton Potato Railway, with Roy Sewell (driver) and Billy Fox. (Len Woodhead)

The railway was also used at 'flitting time', when an employee moved house – one worker remembers how, as a child, he had to share a box van with the family poultry – and for shooting parties on the estate, when a larger carriage, known as the 'Queen Mary' was used to carry the guests.

The Fleet Light Railway was unusual in being built before the First World War, in about 1910, and the equipment was all bought new, rather than second-hand. It extended for about thirteen miles although, for a time, it was linked to another system covering adjacent farms. As well as potatoes, sugar beet and grain, the FLR carried Fenland speciality crops such as celery and strawberries, which were transferred to the M&GN at Fleet station for quick transport to London and other markets.

The potato railways began to fade away during or immediately after the Second World War, when made-up roads allowed better tractors and other vehicles to get into the fields even when wet. The lines also frequently crossed public roads at ungated level crossings, so increasing road traffic made safety a growing concern. The FLR saw two major accidents where it crossed the main A17 trunk road, but since both road drivers were adjudged to have been drunk, no blame was laid on the railway! Despite that, there was pressure to close the lines, and most had gone by the mid 1950s, although a truncated version of the Nocton lines continued in use until 1969.

The temporary nature of the potato railways means that very little survives today. The mill at the station on the Nocton Estate is still standing; there are a couple of pieces of rail embedded in a bridge towards the river; and the gantry across the Witham is still in use by British Sugar. Some rolling stock from the railway was preserved by the Lincolnshire Coast Light Railway, currently being rebuilt near Skegness, and other items went to the now-closed Museum of Army Transport at Beverley.

Nicholas Watt's Vine House Farm at Deeping St Nicholas has a restored wagon on a stretch of rail laid on a transhipment platform, which can be seen by visitors to his farm shop, but that is probably the only visible fragment of the 100-plus miles of the Lincolnshire Potato Railways.

137

Breakers' train collecting sleepers and other equipment as a line is removed.

RAF Cranwell

This five-mile line ran from the GN's Sleaford station to the RAF's Cranwell airfield, and was originally laid in 1917 to carry materials and personnel for the construction of the airfield. The passenger station was close to the main entrance to the camp, but the line also served a coal compound, the boiler house for the main buildings and a number of sidings, one of which ran along Lighter Than Air Road to the airship compounds on the north of the site.

Competition from local bus services saw passenger trains end in 1927, but the line continued to carry goods until 1956, although special trains were run for the Coronation in 1953.

Parts of the line north of the A17 trunk road are still in use as farm roads, with an embankment and overbridge clearly visible from the A15 Leasingham bypass, but it is harder to follow south of the A17, although it can be found again shortly before the junction at Sleaford.

The Lincoln Avoiding Line

The Lincoln Avoiding Line was built as part of the GN&GE Joint line, and carried that line round the city on a high-level embankment, removing the need for through goods trains to go over the heavily congested level crossings on the High Street.

Unfortunately, the line was closed and the embankments removed as part of the reorganisation of Lincoln's railways in the 1980s, just before an increase in rail use led to plans to use the joint line for more goods trains, diverted from the ECML. That increased traffic is now having to use two level crossings, one on the High Street and the other a little to the west, much to the irritation of motorists and pedestrians.

Little can now be seen of the Avoiding Line, which was rapidly levelled and built over in most places. A short stretch of trackbed can be found east of Canwick Road towards the junction with the existing line, and the track is in use west of the city as part of the diverted Midland Railway route into St Mark's.

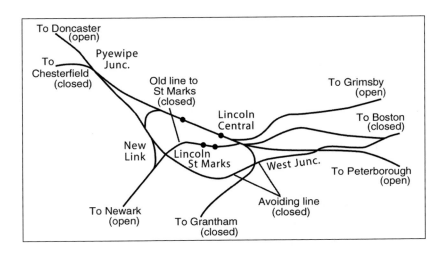

A BR Austerity heavy goods loco takes a train over the river Witham on the Lincoln Avoiding Line. (Peter Grey)

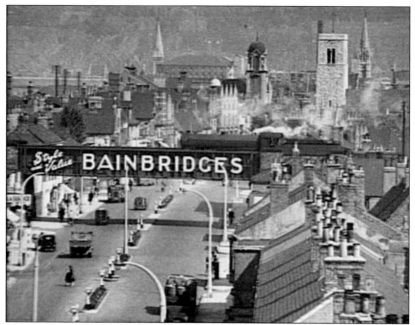

A train crossing the Bainbridge bridge over Lincoln High Street on the Avoiding Line. All traces of the line here are now gone.

Spalding to March

The other casualty of the 1980s was the stretch of the Joint line between Spalding and March, in Cambridgeshire. Opened in 1867 by the GN, it had two stations, at Cowbit and Postland, in Lincolnshire; one right on the county border at French Drove & Gedney Hill; with two more, Murrow and Guyhirne, in Cambridgeshire.

It became part of the Joint line in 1882 and served as such till November 1982, when it was closed to save on rebuilding costs and, ironically, reduce the cost of road improvements at Guyhirne.

The local passenger service on the line was always sparse, but goods traffic was heavy, and the line carried many through

142

Postland station on the Spalding–March line. (Great Northern Railway Society)

trains from the Midlands and the North heading for the ports of the East Coast. Retaining this piece of line would have allowed trains diverted from the ECML a through route from London to Doncaster without having to meet the Main Line at all. Unfortunately, without it, such services now have to run into and out of Peterborough, using ECML track.

Parts of the line can still be found, including the bridge which carried it across the Welland just south of Spalding. The next section has been largely absorbed into farmland, but a link road between the A16 and Clay Lake Bank uses the trackbed, which can then be traced as farm roads or field dividers to the station at Cowbit, where the goods shed and signal box are still intact, though very weathered. The station is a private house.

Field boundaries and stretches of overgrown trackbed can then be followed to the county boundary, passing through the station sites of Postland and French Drove, both of which survive as houses and commercial premises.

143

St Mark's station, Lincoln

St Mark's was Lincoln's first station, the terminus of the Midland line from Nottingham and Newark, later becoming a through station with GC trains going on to Market Rasen, Grimsby and Cleethorpes. It was originally simply named Lincoln, then became Lincoln Midland after the arrival of the GN with its station at Lincoln Central. It was renamed Lincoln St Mark's in 1950, but it remained 'the Midland station' to people like my mother-in-law until the end of its days in 1985.

Direct train services to the capital made it the station of choice for travellers to London and the South, and High Speed Trains, or Inter-City 125s, provided a valuable service to the city for commuters from Grimsby, Lincoln and Market Rasen until the late 1980s.

Class J69 tank No 68605 hustles a goods train through Lincoln St Mark's. The class was introduced by the Great Eastern Railway in 1902, but was still going strong in the 1950s. (R.K. Blencowe)

The station was closed as part of a project to focus services into the city on a single station, the more conveniently located Central. It also released the site, and the large goods yards to the west of it, for shopping development. The main building was Grade 1 listed, and has been rather unsympathetically incorporated into the new complex, with the porticoed main entrance overshadowed by a large store in pastel colours. A small exhibition relating the railway history can be found inside the entrance to one of the stores.

A view of the interior of St Mark's station in the 1950s before the overall roof was removed.

An ex-Midland Railway Johnson 2-4-0 waits at St Mark's station in the 1920s, shortly after the formation of the LMS.

Conclusion

Dr Richard Beeching is often blamed for the wholesale slaughter of Lincolnshire's railway system, and there is no doubt that his axe severed many lines which had the potential to remain as a useful community service, but the reader will realise by now that many others had struggled financially for most of their existence, and could only have survived with massive public funding.

Greater investment in some of the lines could have transformed them, and it is ironic to think back to the sums that British Rail received in support of its services compared to the much larger amounts that now pass from the taxpayers' pocket, through the arcane rail structure resulting from privatisation, to end up in the pockets of city speculators.

Visitors often stand on the platform outside the side door of our home at Woodhall Junction and wax lyrical about the old days, and how the lines should have been retained. Sadly, a route which wound its way between two towns, served by another line, alongside a river bank and serving half a dozen villages, was probably one that could be spared; but the East Lincolnshire, Spalding to March, Boston to Spalding, Lincoln to Grantham and parts of the M&GN all served substantial communities and merited investment and development.

'Bustitution' has failed miserably as a way of providing for those members of the public who don't own a car or who don't have access to one during the working day, and anyone struggling through the traffic on the A17 towards the East Anglian ports can only fantasise about containers of produce on a fast rail service to the continent.

Dreams of re-opening lines are usually frustrated by the way that land was sold after closure. There are places in the county where long stretches of old trackbed still exist, but are forever lost because of bungalows built across the track at every level crossing. Preserving a through route, perhaps as a footpath or bridle way, would have made a lot of sense, and one can even look at the roads that have been built and think, 'Well, that could soon come up if we need the trains back!'.

Most of the major towns of the county are, however, still linked by railway lines, and there are projects which could significantly improve the lot of the traveller. The possibility of a fast service to London, starting at Grimsby and serving Lincoln, Sleaford and Spalding before joining the ECML at Peterborough, or going east to the capital by way of Ely and Cambridge, is regularly talked about. The new East Midlands rail franchise, being introduced at the time of writing, could see improved links to the midlands and north, and we might even see trains in service capable of carrying a Bank Holiday load of people rather than sardines to Skegness.

Lincolnshire's lost railways are probably gone forever, but remnants are still to be seen. This is a beautiful county, and a few hours off the beaten track looking for the last remains of what was once a comprehensive network will be enjoyable as well as informative.

Opening and Final Closure Dates of Lines to Regular Passenger Traffic

Lincolnshire Loop Line
Opened 17 October 1848.
Closed Coningsby Junction to Boston June 1963.
Lincoln to Coningsby Junction October 1970 for passengers,
April 1971 for goods.
Boston to Spalding October 1970.

East Lincolnshire Railway
Opened in stages, beginning March 1848, fully open
October 1848.
Closed Louth to Firsby October 1970; Grimsby to Louth
December 1980.

Ferries and Docks
Grimsby and Immingham Electric Railway
Opened May 1912. Closed July 1961.

Barton and Immingham Railway
Opened May 1911.
Closed to passengers October 1969. Still partially open for
goods, but most lines lifted in 1981.

New Holland and the ferries
Ferries operated from 1830, rail link opened May 1848.
Closed June 1981.

The Horncastle branch
Opened August 1855.
Closed to passengers November 1954 & goods April 1971.

The Spilsby branch
Opened May 1868.
Closed to passengers September 1939, to goods November 1958.

Bardney to Louth
Opened in stages November 1874 – June 1876.
Closed to passengers November 1951. Closed to goods in stages, but final closure February 1960.

Rails to the Seaside
Louth to Mablethorpe
Opened October 1877.
Closed from Louth up to, but not including, Mablethorpe December 1960.

Willoughby to Sutton on Sea
Opened October 1886 extended to Mablethorpe September 1888.
Closed to goods June 1964 and to passengers in October 1970.

The New Line
Opened July 1913. Closed October 1970.

M&GN
Opened in stages. Spalding to Holbeach May 1858; Holbeach to Sutton Bridge July 1862; Spalding to Bourne August 1866; Bourne to Little Bytham in May 1893.
Closure to all traffic in March 1959, although goods services remained from Spalding to Bourne and Sutton Bridge until April 1965.

Stamford Locals
Stamford to Essendine
Opened November 1856.
Stamford East station closed to passengers in March 1957.
Passenger service diverted to Stamford Town, but closed on the branch in June 1959. Goods continued until March 1963.

Bourne to Essendine
Opened May 1860. Closed June 1951.

Over the Trent
Lancashire, Derbyshire & East Coast Railway
Opened November 1896.
Closed to passengers September 1955, goods July 1980.

Manchester, Sheffield & Lincolnshire
Opened August 1850. Closed November 1959.
Re-opened Sykes Junction to Torksey oil terminal January 1966.
Final closure June 1988.

Light Lines by the Trent
Axholme Joint Railway
Opened Marshland Junction to Reedness January 1900.
Reedness to Fockerby and Crowle August 1902. Crowle to
Haxey Junction November 1904 for goods, January 1905 for
passengers. Epworth to Hatfield Moor, goods only
February 1909.
Closed to passengers July 1933. Closed for goods from Epworth
to Haxey Junction February 1956, on the Hatfield branch
September 1963, and the rest of the branch in April 1965.

North Lindsey Light Railway
Opened from Scunthorpe to West Halton September 1906; to
Winteringham and Winteringham Haven July 1907, and on to
Whitton in December 1910.
Passenger service ended in July 1925.
Closure for goods beyond West Halton took place in October
1951. The station there closed in May 1961 and all general
goods traffic ended on July 1964, although ore trains and the
service to Flixborough continued to use parts of the system.

Blocking the Great Eastern
Lincoln to Grantham
Opened April 1867.
Closed November 1965 (passengers 1962).

Sleaford to Bourne

Opened for goods October 1871 and passengers in January the following year.

Closed to passengers in September 1930. Goods continued until July 1956 on the whole line and from Bourne to Billingborough until April 1965.

Other Lost Lines
The Edenham branch

Opened July 1857. Closed by 1873.

Potato railways

Opened at various times in the early 20th century, mostly in the years just after WWI.

Most closed just after WWII, but the last survivor, the Nocton system, continued until 1969.

RAF Cranwell

Opened as contractors' railway 1917, taken over by RAF in April 1918.

Closed to regular passengers 1927, but occasional specials ran until closure and lifting in August 1956.

The Lincoln Avoiding Line

Opened 1882. Closed October 1983.

Spalding to March

Opened for goods April 1867, passengers August 1867.
Closed November 1982.

St Mark's station

Opened August 1846. Closed May 1985.

Bibliography

Lincolnshire has been fortunate in attracting the attention of some very competent railway historians in recent years, and the following have been extremely useful in my research:

Anderson, Paul *Railways of Lincolnshire* (Irwell Press, 1992)

Bates, Chris and Bairstow, Martin *Railways in North Lincolnshire* (Martin Bairstow, 2005)

Cupit, J. and Taylor, W. *The Lancashire, Derbyshire and East Coast Railway* (Oakwood, 1988)

Franks, D. L. *The Stamford and Essendine Railway* (Turntable Enterprises, 1971)

Goode, C. T. *The Great Northern and Great Eastern Joint Railway* (C. T. Goode, 1989)

Goode, C. T. *The Railways of North Lincolnshire* (C. T. Goode, 1985)

King, P. K. and Hewins, D. R. *The Railways around Grimsby, Cleethorpes, Immingham and NE Lincolnshire* (Foxline Publishing)

Ludlam, A. J. *The Lincolnshire Loop Line (GNR) and the River Witham* (Oakwood, 1995)

Ludlam, A. J. *The East Lincolnshire Railway* (Oakwood, 1991)

Ludlam, A. J. *The Spilsby to Firsby Railway* (Oakwood, 1985)

Ludlam, A. J. *The Horncastle and Woodhall Junction Railway* (Oakwood, 1986)

Ludlam, A. J. *Railways to Skegness* (Oakwood, 1997)

Ludlam, A. J. *Railways to New Holland and the Humber Ferries* (Oakwood, 1996)

Ludlam, A. J. *The Louth, Mablethorpe and Willoughby Loop* (Oakwood, 1987)

Ludlam, A. J. *The Louth to Bardney Branch* (Oakwood, 1984)

Oates, G. *The Axholme Joint Railway* (Oakwood, 1961)

Pearson, R. E. and Ruddock, J. G. *Lord Willoughby's Railway* (Willoughby Memorial Trust, 1986)

Rhodes, John *Bourne to Saxby* (KMS Books, 1989)

Rhodes, John *Bourne to Essendine* (KMS Books, 1986)

Rhodes, John *Great Northern Branch Lines to Stamford* (KMS Books, 1988)

Ruddock, J. G. and Pearson, R. E. *The Railway History of Lincoln* (J Ruddock Ltd, 1985)

Squires, Stewart *The Lincoln to Grantham Line via Honington* (Oakwood, 1996)

Squires, Stewart *The Lincolnshire Potato Railways* (Oakwood, 1987)

Squires, Stewart *The Lost Railways of Lincolnshire* (Castlemead, 1988)

Walker, Stephen *The New Line Kirkstead – Little Steeping* (KMS Books, 1985)

Walker, Stephen *Firsby to Wainfleet and Skegness* (KMS Books, 1987)

Walker, Stephen *Great Northern Branch Lines in Lincolnshire* (KMS Books, 1984)

Wright, Neil *Lincolnshire Towns and Industry 1700–1914* History of Lincolnshire Committee, 1982)

Wrottesley, John *The Great Northern Railway, Vols 1,2,3* (Batsford, 1979)

INDEX